Pra...
WO...

"I come into contact with hundreds, ii .... e students each year, and I know firsthand that this is a book that needed to be written. Elizabeth Freedman helps new graduates understand what it really takes to succeed on the job, and shares a wealth of insight, helpful tips, and practical advice in a fresh, funny style that any new graduate will appreciate. I'd recommend *Work 101* to any new hire at our organization."
—Ann Ulett, Campus Recruiting Manager,
PricewaterhouseCoopers, LLP

"This book provides plenty of insights and practical advice to college graduates on the job. From what to wear at work to what not to say to your boss, this book has it all, delivered in a fresh, fun voice to its readers."
—David Roberts, President and CEO, Equity Methods

"Our organization provides human resources support to hundreds of organizations who demand that our professionals hit the ground running. *Work 101* is the blueprint to help them do so, and offers a wealth of insight and practical information to anyone who wants to start any job off on the right foot. I'd recommend this book to any staffing or human resources organization that wants to empower their candidates to succeed in any work environment."
—Jack Mayhew, Chairman, TSi/HRi Companies

"I recommend *Work 101* as a must-have that offers practical advice; this book spells it out and tells it like it really is when it comes to getting a foot in the door and getting ahead on the job."
—Adrian N. Carter, Director of Student Life and Development,
Broward Community College

LEARNING THE ROPES

OF THE WORKPLACE

WITHOUT HANGING YOURSELF

Elizabeth Freedman, M.B.A.

DELTA TRADE PAPERBACKS

WORK 101
A Delta Trade Paperback / April 2007

Published by Bantam Dell
A Division of Random House, Inc.
New York, New York

Book design by Sabrina Bowers

Delta is a registered trademark of Random House, Inc., and the
colophon is a trademark of Random House, Inc.

Library of Congress Cataloging-in-Publication Data
Freedman, Elizabeth.
Work 101 : learning the ropes of the workplace without hanging
yourself / Elizabeth Freedman.
p. cm.
ISBN 978-0-385-34075-5 (trade pbk.)
1. Job hunting. 2. College students—Employment.
3. Success in business. I. Title.
HF5382. 7. F725 2007
650.1—dc22
2007000129

Printed in the United States of America
Published simultaneously in Canada

www.bantamdell.com

BVG 10 9 8 7 6 5 4 3 2

To new professionals everywhere—
may you find happiness and fulfillment in your own careers

Acknowledgments

I am grateful to so many for ensuring the successful outcome of *Work 101*. Many thanks to Talia Cohen—your insights and commitment to this project were instrumental. To Danielle Perez at Bantam Dell—thank you for your expertise, insight, and terrific enthusiasm for *Work 101*, and to Patricia Ballantyne, her assistant, who truly puts the "professional" in New Professional. Many thanks to family, friends, clients, and colleagues for taking the time to read and review chapters from this book, including: David Roberts, Kevin Giglinto, John Micalizzi, Alex Goor, Lauren Schiffman, Alison Clark, and Barbara Limmer. Additional thanks and much appreciation go to the many New Professionals and their managers who agreed to be interviewed for this book, and to even more friends and family members who were informal editors, sounding boards, and nonstop cheerleaders for this effort. Finally, my deepest appreciation for Andrew, the professional who inspires me and so many others every day.

Contents

SECTION II:
Relationships at Work

SECTION III:
You at Work

INTRODUCTION

The Unspoken Rules:
Why Business Savvy Matters
to Your Career

"There's a fine line between clever and stupid."
—Nigel Tufnel, lead guitarist, *This Is Spinal Tap*

EVEN IF YOU HAVEN'T SEEN THE HILARIOUS MOVIE *This Is Spinal Tap,* it's worth mentioning that Nigel Tufnel, one of the lead characters, is about as dumb as a doorknob. But when it comes to learning the ropes at work, this aging, spandex-wearing rocker is right on the money: There really *is* a fine line between clever and stupid, between workplace intellect and ignorance, and ultimately, between career success and setbacks.

For instance, consider Marci, age 24, an entry-level analyst at a top-tier consulting firm. A magna cum laude college graduate, former student government president, and volunteer for Habitat for Humanity, Marci seems like an employer's dream, right? Right . . . except that Marci was recently admonished for her "poor work ethic" and received a less-than-stellar performance review from her boss.

Turns out that Marci had arrived late at the office on a few occasions—only because things had been slow and there hadn't been that much for her to do—and the boss had noticed. Too bad he hadn't also noticed all of the times she'd stayed late at the office, come in early, and answered emails from her laptop at home.

Unfortunately, Marci learned the hard way that most supervisors still want you at your desk by 9:00 am, slow day or not. She didn't know that even though she was terrific 90 percent of the time, it was the other 10 percent that her boss seemed to remember when it came time for her performance review. In other words, she learned that ultimately, there is a very fine line between success and failure in the eyes of her boss—after all, it only took a few late mornings to undo the goodwill she had been working hard to build up for so many months.

The "Fine Lines" of the Workplace

She's not the only one to learn that lesson. The truth is that many of us make mistakes in the early stages of our careers. It isn't until we've been overlooked for an opportunity, passed by for a promotion, or even scolded by a supervisor that we begin to get a clue—but by then, the damage is already done.

The reality is that the workplace is filled with "fine lines"—for instance, when do persistence and follow-up become pesky and irritating to the boss? When is our desire to improve things viewed by our coworkers as a criticism of the status quo or seen as arrogance on our part that we know better than they do? Knowing how to stay on the right side of these, and many other, equations requires an understanding of the rules of the workplace—and how to succeed within them.

What You Don't Say Says Plenty

How can you begin to grasp some of these unspoken rules, and how can you successfully navigate them? Consider *Silent Messages*, a 1971 study conducted by Dr. Albert Mehrabian, a psychologist and UCLA professor and pioneer in the field of verbal and nonverbal communication. What he discovered was that people are influenced less by what we say than by *how* we say it, noting that 93 percent of our impact comes from things other than the words we use.

What does this mean for you and your career? It means that what you don't say—including your dress, appearance, body language, and more—can actually say a lot about you. In fact, it can shout out loud and clear from the mountaintops exactly who you are.

What does your business behavior—including your communication, dress, and interpersonal skills—really say? Does it reinforce who you say you are, or does it reveal something else?

The Problem with Business Know-How

Here's the problem: Unless some kind soul is willing to enlighten you, you often don't know the answers to the questions I've just presented. And as a result, you don't even know that you're making mistakes in the first place. After all, you can't possibly be as clueless as someone who wipes his hands on a tablecloth during a business lunch, or dresses up like a cowgirl for a job interview, for Pete's sake! You're not *that* bad, you tell yourself, so why worry?

More often than not, we never imagine that we could be the ones with the problem. We never think that we're the cocky ones, the annoying ones, the ones who are anything less than fabulous. Whether it's talking too loudly on your cell phone or hogging the left lane on the highway, the reality is that we're remarkably clueless about our own deficiencies—and even more so when it comes to the workplace.

It's time to take responsibility into our own hands and give ourselves the clue that nobody else will. Whether the problem seems small—like the fact that our table manners could use some work—or big—like the fact that we can't seem to get along with our boss or we're rubbing folks the wrong way during a job interview—the key is to identify what isn't working and fix it. After all, with more than 39 million twentysomethings in the United States today, according to the U.S. Census Bureau, there is no shortage of competition, and it's smart to use every opportunity to shine and give yourself an extra edge when it comes to your career. You don't want to lose opportunities because you made people unsure, uncomfortable, or simply grossed them out over lunch at the office.

The Bottom Line on Business Know-How

Can having the inside scoop on business savvy really impact your bottom line? You bet your bottom dollar.

Within organizations, bad business mistakes—from poor communication, to mishandled memos, to inappropriate behavior—can mean disgruntled employees, lawsuits, and a damaged reputation . . . not to mention lost dollars, particularly for those companies that count on their employees to represent them and their brands in the marketplace. Law firms, accounting firms, consulting firms, advertising and PR agencies, and many, many more are selling the unique knowledge and expertise of their employees. When their employees botch things up, that means lost business. And in the $22 billion professional services industry, that can add up very quickly.

The Good News about Business Know-How

The good news is that figuring out what it really takes to succeed at work, like most things, can be learned to a large extent. In fact, if you can walk, talk, and read this very page, chances are you've mastered things much tougher than learning how to write an appropriate email or make small talk with the best of them at a company dinner.

Ultimately, your success on the job will boil down to one simple concept: building trust. When you handle yourself professionally, you help others feel as if they can count on you. You help other people get to know you, like you, and want to help you. When you've got business know-how under control, people will spend less time focusing on your table manners or wardrobe choices, and more time focusing on you. Now, that's more like it.

Get ready to get smart, avoid mistakes, and jump into what it really takes to make your career count. Be warned, though: Some of this stuff can seem downright confusing, especially when you're encouraged to follow up and be persistent when it comes to landing a job or a new project . . . but not to overdo it. It can get tricky, like when we dive into the nuances of how you ask your boss a question (there really is an art to it). And it can get nasty, particularly when we talk about spitting, slobbering, and drunken antics that have been witnessed at many an office holiday party.

But take heart. If you're reading this book, you're smart (obviously!), savvy, and interested in gaining a competitive edge in your career. But no matter how brilliant you may be, we all have things we can learn and ways in which we can improve. After all, you don't want to take the chance that you're the one who needs the breath mint, do you?

Let this book be your guide along your journey. Take notes in the margins, underline anything that seems relevant to your life (unless it's the body odor section, in which case, please go out and buy some deodorant), and, most important, put into practice what you read. The world could use a few more business-savvy superstars. Join us, won't you?

SECTION I

Business Etiquette at Work

UNSPOKEN RULE #1:
HAVE THEM AT HELLO

When It Comes to Making a Great First Impression at Work, Good Things Do Not Come to Those Who Wait

UNSPOKEN RULE #2:
YOUR FORK IS NOT A SHOVEL, YOUR KNIFE IS NOT A SAW

Dazzle Them at Business Lunches, Dinners, and Anyplace Else Where a Fork Is Required

UNSPOKEN RULE #3:
THE WORKPLACE MEETING IS YOUR CAREER'S SECRET WEAPON

Leverage This Opportunity to Showcase Your Strengths to an Audience

UNSPOKEN RULE #1

Have Them at Hello

**When It Comes to Making a Great First Impression at
Work, Good Things Do Not Come to Those Who Wait**

Inside This Chapter:

Master the Five Steps to Hitting the Ground Running
and Impressing Them from the Beginning

- **Step #1**: When It Comes to the Workplace, Think
  Reputation, Not Impression

- **Step #2**: Strong Introductions Count. Have Them at
  Hello!

- **Step #3**: Get Comfortable with Breaking the Ice

- **Step #4**: Outclass the Competition with a Polished,
  Professional Look

- **Step #5**: Create a Long-Term Plan to Ensure
  Ongoing Reputation Success

CONGRATULATIONS! After all that hard work, the 42 rewrites of your résumé, and the hours preparing for interviews, you landed your job. Now, before you get too carried away with the thrill of full-time employment, take a deep breath and put on your thinking cap. You're about to embark on one of life's most exciting and most demanding journeys: the road to creating a great first impression at work.

Step #1:
When It Comes to the Workplace, Think Reputation, Not Impression

When it comes to making a great first impression, think marathon, not sprint. This is contrary to what most of us already know about first impressions: From the minute we meet someone, an impression is formed in our minds—and wham! We've quickly made up our minds about the other person and that's that.

While nobody is denying the power of the first impression, most of us have been wrong once or twice about someone at first glance and, consequently, changed our "impression" entirely. Personally, if I relied solely on my first impressions of others, I'd be out several friends, not to mention a husband. The truth is that at one time or another, the "first" impressions we make of others are actually formed slowly over time, rather than in one brief instant or moment.

Obviously, this isn't always the case, and it doesn't mean you can show up to work looking disheveled because you'll have the chance to make up for it later. Instead, it means that from the minute you came into contact with your company, you began the process of creating a series of impressions that will form your reputation and build your career. From that initial email you sent to a recruiter, to the look of your résumé, to your appearance and demeanor during a job interview, to the thank-you note you sent (or didn't), all of your interactions contribute to the early formation of your workplace rep, and it just keeps forming from there.

Think Reputation, Not Impression

Like an early impression, a reputation is often built on what seem like little things over time, including your appearance and your overall professionalism. Believe it or not, this is good news, because it really puts you in the driver's seat, where you can take consistent action over time to earn your reputation, as opposed to having the world think less of you because you happen to be having a little trouble with your table manners or ability to make small talk one night at a company dinner.

However, a word of caution: Once your reputation is formed, it's formed. It tends to last for a long time and is tough to change, so take the time to create a reputation you'll be proud of. Think about the millions of dollars McDonald's has spent recently trying to shift its image and reputation in light of a backlash in the marketplace against fattening foods and America's obesity epidemic. Consider the millions more it spent on creating "healthy" new prod-

ucts—like salads and a walnut-and-yogurt snack—to reinforce this new image in your mind. Now let me ask you—did
it work? Have their image and reputation changed dramatically in *your* mind? I don't know about you, but if I'm going
to McDonald's, I'm not going to even pretend I'm eating
something healthy. Bring on the fries!

Who cares, anyway?
Why all the fuss about this reputation stuff? After all, isn't it
the quality of our work that really counts when it comes to
success on the job?

Nobody would argue with the fact that your ability to do
your job well goes a long way at work. But in order for people to take the time to recognize your capabilities and see
the great work you're actually performing, they've got to
trust you first. Think about it: If you wanted to buy a car, you
wouldn't buy one from just anybody, would you? Chances
are that you'd ask around, do your homework, and check
out a few places before you made any real decisions. I doubt
you'd give your hard-earned cash to someone who seemed
sketchy, or unprofessional, or just rubbed you the wrong
way. Why bother, when there are plenty of car dealers to
choose from?

The same goes for you at work. When it comes time for
promotions, bigger bonuses, and plum assignments, people
will ask around, do their homework, and check out their options before handing you the golden ticket. There is plenty
of room for excellence, but the reality is that great opportunities are always limited to a few on the job (there is only
one CEO, after all!). When your reputation is strong, you become the person other people know about, think of, and
want to do business with. In short, you don't give anyone
any reason to hand the prize over to someone else.

How to Build Your Great Reputation

How can you create a series of great impressions that will last in the minds of others? Think of the first six months on the job as one long audition, where everything that you do, say, and wear can contribute to—or detract from—the overall strength of your reputation. This doesn't mean that Big Brother is watching you (well, he is, sort of, but we'll get to that later when we talk about email), and it doesn't mean that once those first six months are up you can start showing up to work at noon. Instead, consider these essential steps to building a strong, professional reputation, one day at a time.

Step #2:
Strong Introductions Count.
Have Them at Hello!

If you've seen the movie *Jerry Maguire,* then you probably remember a romantic scene between the lead characters toward the end of the movie. Just as sports agent Jerry Maguire, played by Tom Cruise, finally declares his love for his assistant (played by Renée Zellweger), she stops him in his tracks and says: "You had me at hello."

When it comes to starting off on the right foot at work, you've got to have them at hello, too. In today's workplace, people are busy and stretched for time with a to-do list that's higher than Mount Everest. As a result, your opportunities to impress, make a splash, or even get someone to remember your name are extremely limited, so you'll want to make the most of these early moments. And it all starts with hello.

Your Introduction:
Saying Hello the Workplace Way

Here's the mistake many of us make at work: We wait for people to introduce themselves to us instead of the other way around. We're the new kid on the block, so we hesitate and become tentative and shy as we try to get to know people around the office. Many of us assume that we'll meet everyone eventually, so what's the rush? Don't be fooled: While you're sitting back and waiting for folks to come to you, the go-getter in the cubicle next door is shaking hands and kissing babies. Plus, waiting around to introduce yourself can get awkward at times, particularly when you've passed the same guy in the hall about 50 times and you still haven't said hello.

Here's the real problem with waiting for people to come to you: When you wait too long, you risk limiting your circle of contacts and networks on the job, despite the fact that these are the very people who might wind up helping you and your career in big ways down the road. When it comes to this step, good things do *not* come to those who wait. Instead, grab the bull by the horns, take a deep breath, and start to meet and greet the workplace way.

Dos and Don'ts
for Introducing Yourself at Work

DO *TAKE YOUR TIME WHEN YOU START INTRODUCING YOURSELF AROUND THE OFFICE.* Yes, I want you to grab the bull by the horns, but I don't want you to scare anyone, either. No sending out emails to everyone in the company to say hello or anything else along those lines. Rome wasn't built in a day, and neither is your ability to meet everyone at work within a week on the job. When it comes to introductions, one at a time is best.

DO *REMEMBER THAT WHEN IT COMES TO MEETING FOLKS AROUND THE OFFICE,* one size does not fit all. In some cases, sending out an introductory email may be appropriate, and in other cases, you will need to meet and greet in person. In other instances, you may want to ask a coworker to coffee or lunch, or agree to meet up at an office event or conference. How to know which mode is right? While there aren't any hard-and-fast rules, one approach is to start small and work up from there. For example, you could send an introductory email to say hello, and follow up a few weeks later with an invitation to coffee.

DO *MAKE A LIST OF PEOPLE IN THE OFFICE THAT YOU'D LIKE TO MEET AND INTRODUCE YOURSELF TO.* Make this list as long as it needs to be—don't edit yourself by thinking that you'll never get to meet Mr. Bigwig or Ms. Hotshot. The truth is that you may not meet senior-level executives for a while—but that's fine. This list is a work in progress, and as you get more familiar with people and office politics, you may add or delete a name or two. If you're not sure whom to put on your list, think strategically: Who seems like they are on the fast track at work? Who has a strong expertise in a certain area? Who has worked for the company for a while? Who is well liked? Look for clues to guide you.

DO *HAVE YOUR BOSS HELP YOU COME UP WITH THIS LIST.* Ask her, *"If you were making a list of people to* *meet at work, who would go on it and why?"* Don't be afraid to periodically enlist your boss to help you meet others on your list, too. The key word here is *periodically*: Your boss is in the business of getting things done, not of getting your network up and running, so don't overwhelm her with requests.

DON'T *ASSUME THAT YOUR BOSS WILL DO THE INTRODUCING FOR YOU.* If he or she does introduce you around the office—either by literally taking you by the hand and introducing you to the folks on your floor, or by sending out an email to the team—that's great, and that's what a good boss should do. If not, don't be afraid to drop a hint or two to the boss. You might ask: *"I'd like to get to know some of the people around the office that I'll be working closely with. Are there a few people that you could introduce me to?"*

DON'T *FORGET TO FULLY LEVERAGE THE POWER OF YOUR LIST.* Once you've met with someone, simply ask him or her, *"Do you happen to know Alyssa in research? Would you be willing to introduce me to her?"* One note: Even if people are nice enough to help introduce you around the office, don't expect them to do all the work for you. After they've promised to introduce you to Alyssa, send a friendly reminder email with a draft of a written introduction they could provide on your behalf if needed.

DON'T *ASSUME THAT YOUR LIST OF WHOM TO MEET EVER GOES AWAY.* You've heard the old expression: *It's not what you know, it's who you know.* You will always need the help of others to grow your career and skills;

therefore . . . *it's not what you know, it's who you know* and *who knows you, too.* As long as you eat, breathe, and watch bad TV, please, please, keep adding to your list and working on it.

As you can see, there is more to an introduction than meets the eye. That's because an introduction isn't just about saying hi to a coworker at the water cooler; it's really about establishing a foundation with someone who can impact your career. If the foundation is weak from the beginning, chances are you aren't going to build the kind of relationships you might like to have—or need to have—down the road.

This isn't to sound scheming or Machiavellian, to suggest that relationships aren't a two-way street or that we don't also meet people for fun, friendship, and so on. It also doesn't mean that we're going to be thick as thieves with everyone we meet, or that we'll even wind up connecting with all the people we reach out to. Nonetheless, making the effort to know people from the very beginning of your career will deliver results down the road for you. The truth is that most of us don't bother to reach out, we don't do the work to establish and maintain strong professional networks, and most of us really, really wish that we had when the you-know-what hits the fan. Just ask anyone who has ever lived through downsizing or layoffs, or who needed a job, a referral, new clients, funding for a new business, or anything else. Think of relationships as the gas for your career car— you simply can't get where you need to go without them.

Step #3:
Get Comfortable with Breaking the Ice

Now that you've determined whom you want to meet, it's time to get to the how. For many of us, it's one thing to know we want to meet the manager down the hall, but it's entirely another issue to actually get up out of our chair and do it. No matter how great an idea this may have seemed at the time, we all go through moments of self-doubt when it comes to taking risks, even for something as innocent as an introduction. Courage, my friend!

If you'd like to meet a few folks at the office, particularly those who fall outside of your immediate circle, remember the phrase that pays: Less is more, so no need to go into email overdrive. Instead, consider a few simple ways to break the ice around the office:

Top Five Tips for Breaking the Ice around the Office

Tip #1: Before you send an email or shake a hand, have a goal in mind. In other words, why do you want to meet this person? For instance, if you want to meet Jan because she's the marketing "guru" around the office, you might say in an email: *"Jan, I've heard so much about your expertise in marketing, and I'm hoping you might be willing to share a few thoughts with me."* When you have a reason to call or write, it makes things seem more natural and comfortable for you both.

Tip #2: Pretend that you are meeting you for the first time. How do you look? How are you dressed? And, to be blunt, how do you smell? I know you're gorgeous and smell delicious, but why take a chance? Let's face facts: There are dozens of brands of breath mints and deodorants on the market today—somebody has got to need these things. Ask a close friend to give you an honest assessment of how you really come across at a first glance. I don't care how great you are—if your breath stinks or you smell, it just grosses people out.

Tip #3: I know you've said hi a million times, so you don't need an instruction manual on the topic . . . or do you? The truth is that many of us ruin a perfectly good hello with a weak handshake, sweaty palms, bad breath, poor eye contact, and no smiles. Don't assume you aren't guilty of any of these. How to be sure? Once again, this is where having a trusted friend to practice on comes in handy. At the very least, practice in the mirror: Try saying *"Hi, I'm _____. It's great to meet you"* a few times. No matter how confident you might feel on the inside, a weak introduction definitely says otherwise.

Tip #4: Think of an introduction as a giving, rather than a getting, exchange, during which you offer something to someone else as a means of saying hello. If you come across an interesting article in the *Wall Street Journal* (which you read on a regular basis, naturally), clip it out and send it along with a casual note to the sales director down the hall with a message like *"Hi, John, we haven't met, but I work with Jim in*

Product Management. Heard that you were doing some work with Citibank, and thought this article might be of interest." I'm not suggesting you spend your days subscribing to every periodical under the sun and clipping out articles. If nothing else, this "giving" strategy—whether you're offering homemade cookies or an interesting book—provides you with a great excuse to say hello to someone. And when you offer something that actually has real meaning to that other person, they will remember and appreciate you for it.

Tip #5: Because people are busy and rely so heavily on email, your first introduction to someone may very well be through a computer. In that case, make sure your email is short, sweet, and to the point: *"Hi, John. We haven't met, but I've recently joined Jim's team and I wanted to introduce myself. I'm excited about the fact that we'll be working together on several upcoming projects, and if there is anything that I can do for you or your team, please don't hesitate to let me know."* Keep your message positive, and don't be afraid to ask for something: *"I know how busy you must be, but if you've got a few minutes, I'd love to stop by your office to learn about some of the outreach initiatives coming up in the next few months."* Don't forget that an email is you, on a computer screen, so look sharp: Always check for typos, grammatical mistakes, or misspelled words before you press send.

What's the moral of the introduction story? Be prepared. Whether you're trying to meet someone or you simply bump into a coworker down the hall, be ready to make the most of this moment. The truth is that a strong handshake, the ability to make small talk (which we'll discuss in greater detail in Chapter Three, but let's just say for now that it goes way beyond talking about the weather), and the way you connect with people will pay real dividends down the road. Whether you are presenting yourself to others at a new job, a cocktail party, a conference, or a meeting, the goal is always the same: to create connections with other people. When you put your best foot forward, you put other people at ease. Even better, you increase the chances that other people will enjoy your company and want to spend even more time with you. Now, *that's* an introduction.

Step #4:
Outclass the Competition with a Polished, Professional Look

I once heard someone describe the importance of wearing the right workplace attire by comparing it to buying a bar of soap: If you needed to buy a bar of soap and you had to choose between soap that was packaged nicely in a pretty box and soap that was packaged in a crumpled box with ripped-up packaging, which would you choose? Even if the product is the same quality bar of soap, we go for the appealing packaging, every time.

When it comes to your appearance and attire at work, you're just like that bar of soap. If your packing is yucky, crumpled up, or otherwise unappealing, you're not doing yourself any favors. This doesn't mean that you have to spend a fortune on a work wardrobe or look like Brad Pitt in order to win over your coworkers. But let's not pretend that people don't care about the packaging, because we all do, down to the bar of soap we buy in the store. This may seem superficial or unfair, but don't fight it. Don't complain about how a certain look isn't you or that you should have the right to dress as you please. Listen, I'm on your side, and that's why the goal is simply to choose attire that's appropriate, professional, and keeps the focus where it should be: on your ability to perform the job. You aren't just representing you anymore—you're also representing a company and what it stands for, and we don't want what you wear to get in the way of that.

What Is Business Casual, Anyway?

My first job out of graduate school was working for a global consulting firm where strict business attire was required four days a week. As much as some people would hate having to wear a suit most days, many of us at the company were relieved by the rule. You simply woke up in the morning, pulled on a suit, and you were all set. No fuss, no muss.

However, my morning routine would shatter to pieces every Friday, when the firm permitted business casual attire. Suddenly, my quick routine turned into a lengthy process of figuring out what I could wear, what I could get away with, and what I'd get shot modeling in the workplace. Judging by the appearances of my coworkers each Friday, I wasn't the only one who was confused: Some wore khaki pants, others wore jeans, and I noticed a few pairs of flip-flopped feet, as we were all trying to figure out exactly what was kosher. Fortunately, our Human Resources Department didn't leave us floundering for long, and a list of guidelines for business casual attire was instituted soon enough. Gone were the flip-flops, jeans, and plenty of other things, too. In fact, there were so many rules that many of us just went back to wearing our suits: It was boring, but at least we knew what we were doing.

Say Goodbye to the Suit:
Business Casual Isn't Going Anywhere

So, what are you supposed to wear to work these days? Most of the time, we're told to follow a business casual dress code. While some recent articles have heralded the return of the suit to the workplace, the truth is that many of us only wore a suit to work on the day we interviewed for the job. While you might wear a suit for a big presentation, a meeting with clients, or some other big deal at work, chances are that you're in the same business casual boat as the rest of us, at least most of the time. Add to that the fact that business casual is actually a very broad term that means "anything but a suit," and now you're in for a real treat. With terms like "office casual," "corporate casual," "executive business casual," and more, you can see how confusion reigns supreme when it comes to the work wardrobe.

Putting the "Business" Back in
Business Casual

The problem with business casual is that many of us put the emphasis on the word "casual," instead of "business," which is where it belongs. Originally, business casual attire was offered by companies as a way for employees to get away from wearing a suit and tie, not as an opportunity to put on flip-flops, a pair of low-rise jeans, or a baseball cap at work. (I once did a training program for a group of new employees at a large accounting firm, and the attire for the program was business casual. A new hire, wearing a baseball cap, was *thrown out of the program and sent home to change* by the human resources director for not following the rules. His exact words to the employee: "If you can't follow some obvious rules about attire, how can I expect you to handle a meeting with a client?" Ouch.)

The Problem with Business Casual

The problem with a business casual dress code is that the code may differ depending on the business you work in, for whom you work, or simply what time of year it is, so the hard-and-fast rules are actually pretty slippery and loose. The bottom line is that what business casual attire means to you, your coworkers, or even your boss—let alone the director of HR at your company—may differ greatly. Save yourself some time and trouble and simply find out what the rules are at your specific organization. Hopefully this information was shared with you at your company orientation, if your company offered one, or it's somewhere in that employee handbook of yours. Get acquainted with the rules, so that you know what's what.

But as always, there are the written rules and then there are the unspoken ones. Just because your office handbook doesn't explicitly state "No bright purple pants allowed," it doesn't take a rocket scientist to figure out that the funky-colored pants stay in the closet.

What NOT to Wear:
Better Safe than Sorry

Sure, you might work for the most laid-back office on the planet where you could show up in your underwear and not turn a head. In that case, skip the next part of this book.

Otherwise, consider our list below of what not to wear to work, no matter how tempted you might be. Keep this in mind: When it comes to dressing for the office, our mantra is "better safe than sorry." These guidelines are definitely on the conservative side, and may not apply to every workplace, but when it comes to building a reputation, why take a chance?

The Rules—Spoken and Unspoken— for Business Casual Attire

1. *FOOTWEAR, PART I:* NO flip-flops! I don't care if they cost you $100 and are adorned with jewels from Tiffany, just don't do it. The flip-flop simply screams "I'd rather be sunbathing at the pool" to the world. There isn't anything remotely businesslike or professional about them, so save them for the surf.

   (Special note for walkers or for those of you who have to hoof it around town: Make sure that if you are wearing flip-flops or other excessively casual footwear as you walk from the train or subway to the office, you change your shoes as soon as you arrive at work. Nobody is expecting you to act like Superman and change in the nearest phone booth before you arrive in the lobby of your office building, but don't wait until after you settle in, chat with a coworker or two, get your coffee, and check your emails to spruce up, either. One partner at a large accounting firm complained about how she frequently saw employees in the elevator or around the water cooler wearing flip-flops as they went through their morning routine. She wasn't impressed, and neither were the clients who also witnessed the footwear—after all, the clients didn't know that the flip-flops were going to be swapped for something more professional. The moral of the story? Footwear counts and people do notice, so plan accordingly.)

While you're at it, watch out for sandals and other open-toed shoes in the summer. If your office does permit them, choose sandals that are on the conservative side (no spiky heels, funky colors, or platform shoes), and make sure the feet look pretty. Don't gross us out with your icky toenails and scaly heels, please. (That goes for the guys, too.)

2. *FOOTWEAR, PART II:* When it comes to wearing sneakers, tread carefully. Often, if you are allowed to wear jeans to the office, you can wear sneakers, too, but don't assume that's the policy. And, ladies, keep the shoes professional. Teetering around in five-inch heels or clomping around the water cooler in your chunkiest pair just doesn't fit the bill. And no slippers, Chinese, bedroom, or otherwise. And in case I don't sound enough like your mother, do not, repeat, do not wear sandals with socks to work. That's just bad fashion. Speaking of socks, guys, be sure that the dress socks you wear come up to midcalf or your knees, so that when you sit, we don't get a glimpse of bare skin.

3. *REMEMBER, YOU AREN'T THE EXCEPTION TO THE DRESS CODE RULE, WHATEVER THAT RULE MIGHT BE.* David, a mathematician, described how one employee of his often sported the sandal-sock look. Even worse, this same colleague took off his sandals and socks and walked around the office *barefoot.* Here's the best part: *He used to type on his keyboard with his feet, barefoot!* Horrid beyond belief.

Why did David let the employee get away with such revolting footwear (or lack thereof)? The explanation: "He was completely brilliant. We could have gotten rid of him, but honestly, we just couldn't find another mathematician with his unique set of skills. So we tried to get him to change, and in the meantime, we put up with his eccentricities." Unless you are a brilliant mathematician, have discovered the cure for cancer, or are Bill Gates in disguise, forget about making your own dress code rules. We know that you wouldn't ever pull a move like our fair-footed mathematician, but in our own way, many of us think we are the exception to the rule and that we can wear what we want. Often it's because we're dying to wear that special something, or because we're convinced that we're not idiots and what we've got on is cute, fashionable, or simply acceptable. Remember that dressing for work isn't about standing out for your amazing fashion sense; it's about showing you've got good judgment and setting the right tone.

4. *IT'S NOT JUST WHAT YOU WEAR, IT'S HOW YOU WEAR IT.* Clothes should be crisp, pressed, and neat, so get rid of the khaki pants with the frayed edges around the bottom or the shirt that always seems to look wrinkled. (If you hate ironing as much as I do, invest in a few pairs of wrinkle-resistant shirts and pants and save yourself time and trouble.) Polish the shoes (and your nails—no chipped nail polish!), replace the missing buttons, and don't sport anything with stains, rips, or other signs of wear and tear. While we're at it, no stockings, tights, or panty hose with runs, no worn-down heels, and please, nothing that you haven't washed really, really recently. Sure, you may have to spend a couple of extra bucks on dry cleaning, but think of it this way: If you happen to bump into the CEO in the hall, you want to look sharp and crisp, not wrinkled and rumpled.

5. *AVOID EXTREMES.* Anything that is too tight or too short is automatically out, and likewise, keep the baggy, the extreme, and the too long for your time off. Too "jingly" is also distracting, so avoid jewelry that makes noise, dangles, or otherwise seems excessive. And, guys, keep the earrings and other jewelry (other than a wedding ring and maybe a simple bracelet) at home. Unless you're Tony Soprano, the pinky ring simply doesn't belong at the office.

Finally, too high or too low (think of midriff-baring shirts and low-rise jeans) should be kept out of the workplace. Yes, low-rise pants are still the rage these days, and some of you have spent big bucks on low-rise jeans, but you and I know there is low and then there is *low.* If a coworker can see that you're wearing a thong or what God gave you, it's too low, and let's just leave it at that. Last but not least: No cleavage! Keep the low-cut sweaters and blouses for another time. As image consultant Mary Lou Andre, author of *Ready to Wear: An Expert's Guide to Choosing and Using Your Wardrobe,* puts it, "More skin, less power."

6. *IF BUSINESS CASUAL IS A YEAR-ROUND POLICY AT YOUR OFFICE,* then don't get too relaxed in the summer when it comes to dress. Wear a shirt with a collar, not a T-shirt, and keep the capris and other summer pants at home unless they come down below the calf. Hawaiian shirts are out, and be careful about wearing sleeveless tops and revealing bare legs—many offices have policies against these. No sunglasses indoors, no sports jerseys, and no music headphones. While you're at it, skip the sundresses, bare shoulders, halter tops, shorts, spaghetti-strap tops, and anything else that might show off a bra strap or two. Trust me, if your coworkers know what

color your bra is, you're wearing the wrong outfit to work. Finally, no hats allowed, unless wearing a head covering is in line with your particular religious practice.

7. *USE YOUR BEST JUDGMENT WHEN IT COMES TO PERFUMES AND COLOGNES.* Personally, I can't get enough of the stuff, but many people are sensitive to it and are too polite to tell you that your Obsession is giving them a migraine. If you know you're spending your day with others in a small, confined space—such as a meeting room or office—go light on the fragrance or skip it altogether.

8. *LOOK BETTER THAN YOU HAVE TO.* You've heard the old adage "Dress for the job you want, not for the job you have." Many people resist stepping up their work wardrobe, offering reasons like "I sit behind a desk all day and nobody sees me anyway," or "I don't visit clients—all my work is done in front of a computer." Don't kid yourself. People—including your boss—see you plenty, and they notice your appearance (and everything else, too, from what you eat, to what you do online, to when you arrive and leave—and more!). When you make the effort to look the part, you broadcast to the world that you are the kind of person who takes yourself and the job seriously. Don't underestimate how many people will notice that.

9. *DETAILS COUNT.* For men, that means facial hair is kept in line (no stubble, please), and clean nails are a must for everyone. Hair is clean, neat, and no dandruff—that's why God invented Head & Shoulders shampoo. Get rid of the piercings, unless you want to work at a record store, and cover up exposed tattoos. Leave backpacks and other book bags for school, and make an investment

WORK 101   31

in a quality leather portfolio, leather bag, or other kind of
briefcase instead. Whatever bag you choose, make sure it
isn't too worn-out or beat-up looking, and get rid of the
wacky buttons or political stickers that might cover it.
Ladies, a purse is fine, but no canvas or straw bags,
please.

10. *UNLESS YOU'RE TOLD OTHERWISE, JEANS ARE NOT CONSID-
ERED BUSINESS CASUAL ATTIRE.* Some offices will allow
jeans on special occasions or casual Fridays—but otherwise, don't assume that jeans are part of your company's
dress code.

Annoyed? Too many rules for you? Overly picky? Maybe
so, but when it comes to what you wear at work, I want you
to have all the information at your fingertips, so that you
don't make mistakes that could easily have been avoided.
Remember what was said earlier: It's hard to fix a damaged
reputation, and nothing sinks your own reputation faster
than dressing inappropriately or unprofessionally. I'm not
suggesting that wearing the right clothes will land you the
promotion, the great assignments, or the big raise. But *not*
presenting the right image may very well stand in your way
of the good things at work. After all, how many senior-level
executives do you know who walk around looking sloppy,
unprofessional, and inappropriate?

So, What Can I Wear?

Depending on where you work, you'll find a different set of
guidelines for what constitutes business casual dress, as we
stated earlier. For that reason, you won't find a list of
specifics about what to wear here, because what you should
wear is really determined by the specific culture in your

workplace. Some of you might work in very casual environments where anything goes, or in small offices with only two or three employees where dress isn't a big issue. Still, we don't want anyone showing up to work nude, so keep a few suggestions in mind. One final note—these tips are geared to a more corporate work environment. If that isn't you, take the suggestions that work and leave the rest behind.

- *NOT SURE WHAT TO WEAR?* Ask your boss. Even if you observe what your boss wears on a regular basis, don't be afraid to ask *"What are you wearing when we visit the client tomorrow?"* Or simply say: *"I was planning to wear X and Y to the client tomorrow. Does that work?"* (**Helpful hint:** Ladies, if you've got a male boss, you may want to ask a female counterpart. No disrespect to the men, but talking about clothing with their younger female subordinates makes many a male boss uncomfortable or, at the very least, unsure about what to say or not to say.)

- *LOOK AROUND.* If you're the only one showing up to work in a tie or dress suit, you may want to tone it down. After all, if you want to be on the team, wear the team uniform. Dress in a style that seems to be in line with what other folks are doing.

- *DON'T TRY TO GET AWAY WITH ONE WARDROBE.* Many of us wear the same things to work that we wear on the weekend—but business casual is not casual dress. It's an upscale, professional dress code, not to be confused with what you wear out with your friends.

- *WHEN IN DOUBT, WEAR A BLAZER OR JACKET.* It's an easy way to look professional and polished without a lot of work. Because many of us work in fast-paced, unpredictable jobs, you never know when you're going to be called on to meet with a client, so keep a jacket hanging in your cubicle at work, too, so you're ready to look sharp anytime.

What's THONG with This Picture?

I recently worked with a client who told me about Green Jeans, an employee who liked to wear tight green jeans to the office on a regular basis, despite the fact that jeans and tight clothing were strictly prohibited in the company's business casual dress code. Everyone noticed this employee's tight clothing— hence the nickname she was given. For all I know, Green Jeans may have been smart, talented, and capable (in fact, I assume she was; otherwise, she wouldn't have a job at this top firm), but that wasn't what she was known for around the office. She was known for what she wore.

Like it or not, women have to pay extra attention to wardrobe choices in the office. Between revealing thong un- derwear, tight shirts, and short skirts, women have to watch out for wearing stuff that is inappropriate. It may seem unfair, but we are judged for how we look and how we dress, and the fact is that our contributions will not be the first thing people notice or remember about us if we're letting our cleavage do the talking.

Sexy and professional just don't mix, and even if you are young, cute, and single, the goal isn't to land a date at work. I'm sure you look fine, but if you receive feedback or hints that tell you otherwise, be open to changing what you wear so that people focus on *you*, not your wardrobe. As one partner at an accounting firm told me, "I had a meeting recently, where the men showed up in button-down shirts and khaki pants and the women showed up in revealing clothing. After the meeting, I remembered what the men said, and I remembered what the women wore. It shouldn't be that way." What are you known for at work—your ideas or your wardrobe?

Step #5:
Create a Long-Term Plan to Ensure Ongoing Reputation Success

Whether it's figuring out what to say or wear during the first months on the job, one thing by now is very clear: A polished, professional workplace reputation doesn't just happen on its own. Instead, it's something that is created and managed by you, and requires thought, effort, and plenty of time and attention. But your work isn't over yet.

Unfortunately, a reputation isn't something that we can just put on autopilot. Think of it like that car we mentioned earlier. You've bought the car, but to keep it running, you'll need to take it into the shop every so often for repairs, maintenance work, and so on. Your reputation is the same way: Now that you've laid some great groundwork, it's important to do the upkeep and monitoring to keep it operating smoothly.

What does it really take to keep your reputation where you want it? If you want to stay on the success track that you've begun to carve out for yourself, keep the following Dos and Don'ts in mind:

Dos and Don'ts for
Keeping Your Reputation on Track

DO *STAY THE COURSE*. To put it another way, if it ain't broke, don't fix it. If you've found a successful strategy for meeting new people at work or for keeping your image polished and fresh, then certainly keep on doing what you've been doing. The problem people run into is that they start to settle in to work, get too comfortable in their routine, and the next thing you know, they're wearing flip-flops to the office.

DO *COME UP WITH NEW WAYS TO REACH OUT TO NEW COLLEAGUES*. Offer to give a presentation at an internal company event or help run a meeting for your boss. Join the office softball team, help run a canned food drive—anything to broaden your circle of contacts and develop more experience.

DO *WORK ON CONTINUOUSLY IMPROVING YOUR OWN SKILLS AND TALENTS*. If you'd like to start giving presentations at the office, why not join a local Toastmasters club to get the practice and experience you'll need? If you know that your office is expanding to Mexico, take a course in Spanish at a local community college or language school. (Who knows? Your company may even pay for it.)

DO *JOIN A PROFESSIONAL ASSOCIATION*, go to a conference, or attend a seminar to learn about sales, marketing, or anything else that might make you more valuable to your boss and company. Make a list of how you might begin to improve a skill, learn something new, or gain experience in a new area. Stretched for time? As the motivational speaker Zig Ziglar likes to say, "Enroll in Automobile University." You can buy audiobooks (or get them free from your local library) that will teach you anything from finance to fishing— simply pop a CD into your car and learn while you drive; if you travel by bus or subway, you can use your iPod or other mp3 player to listen to podcasts downloaded from the Internet on any subject of interest.

DO *KEEP ASKING YOURSELF QUESTIONS SO THAT YOU KNOW WHERE TO PUT YOUR EFFORT NEXT.* Focus on things like:

> Whom do I want to meet over the next six months?
>
> What are the top three skills I'd like to develop over the next year?
>
> What is the next company event, conference, or workshop that I'd like to attend?
>
> What are three projects I'd like to play a role in before the end of the year?
>
> What are five things I can do each week to make my boss's life easier?
>
> What are three things I can do to help my company become more competitive in the marketplace?

DON'T *FORGET THAT YOU STILL HAVE A JOB TO DO.* If your work performance isn't up to snuff, no reputation, no matter how strong, will save you. Thinking and planning for your career beyond the tasks in front of you is critically important, but not at the expense of poor or shoddy work.

DON'T *REST FOR TOO LONG ON YOUR LAURELS.* If you made a big splash during the first few weeks or months at work, that's something to be proud of. But remember: The workplace has a short memory, and you've got to keep on proving yourself, no matter how terrific you were six months ago. Think about it: You don't necessarily care whether your car worked beautifully a year ago. You want to make sure it's still working today when you have to go somewhere.

It's Your Attitude that Keeps Your Reputation Going in the Right Direction

As cliché as it sounds, attitude is everything when it comes to starting off—and staying—on the right foot at work. You probably know a lot about what it takes to have a great attitude, so when it comes to the workplace, apply what you know in terms of the choices you make. As the employees of Seattle's Pike Place Fish Market say, "Choose Your Attitude," putting their own technique for having fun at work into practice. After all, it's one thing to say you've got a great attitude, it's another thing to show it.

How's Your Attitude?
A Few Simple Ways to Show You Care

* *ATTITUDE DETERMINES WHETHER YOU SHOW UP TO WORK EARLY OR LATE,* leave when the clock strikes 5:00 pm or stay until you're done. No one is suggesting you have to work around the clock, but putting in the time to get the

job done is part of building the reputation you want. Arriving late and leaving early is not, and that goes double for calling in sick when you're not.

- **"WORK HARD AND SHOW THAT YOU CARE ABOUT THE JOB,"** says Dale Kalman, vice president of stock plan services for Charles Schwab. Adds Kalman, "There has been a trend of a lack of work ethic among some of the younger employees that I've noticed. We've had some all-stars, definitely, but I've seen employees who come in late frequently, or don't come in at all and don't call us or let us know ahead of time that this will be the case. That gives a strong impression of just not caring, and it's not going to win you any points."

- *HOW DO YOU HANDLE THE UNEXPECTED?* Deb, who had recently joined a new team at a large financial services firm, was excited about her new, more senior position. Two days into her new role, the administrative assistant quit, and Deb and her teammates were left with weeks of data entry to perform. Suck it up, or complain about it? Deb chose the former, and also chose to keep things in perspective. We all have to do more than our fair share of filing, stapling, or making copies from time to time, so when it comes to doing grunt work, forming a good reputation means you smile and deal with it. So the next time you're handed a pile of copies to make, borrow the line that the actor Kevin Bacon uses in *Animal House* while getting whacked in the derriere at a fraternity ritual: "Thank you, sir, may I have another?" Even better, try this one on: "Is there anything else that I can do for you?"

- *FROM THE MOMENT YOU STARTED WORK,* you may have received suggestions, advice, or feedback from your boss or other senior colleagues. Did you really listen to it, ignore it, or get defensive? The best reputations are built on listening to constructive criticism and then asking the following questions: "What can I learn from this? How will I use this information to improve?" Take it one step further, and actively get the feedback you need to learn and grow, even if no one offers it to you. Use that great attitude of yours and ask your boss: "Do you have any suggestions for how I might improve this report for next month?"

- *YOUR ATTITUDE IS REFLECTED EVERYWHERE,* from how long you take for lunch, to what you do on your computer besides business-related tasks, to how you expense items, to abusing the phone. Remember, employers do notice what you do, and even if they didn't, your reputation is about showing integrity and honesty in everything that you do. "Some of the younger employees I know definitely take it easy," says Tina Reejsinghani, an assistant brand development manager for one of the world's largest consumer products companies. "If people know the boss is away for the day, you'll see some of them come in late or leave early because they think nobody will notice."

- *ATTITUDE ABOUT WORK IS REFLECTED EVERYWHERE,* even if you're far away from the office. Just ask the employee who bad-mouthed her boss on a personal blog. Can you guess what happened next? Not only did her boss read the blog, he forwarded it to HR, who canned her. Employees at companies like Starbucks, Delta Air Lines, Google, Microsoft, and many more have been fired because of their blogging practices. Whether it's through a blog or something you post on MySpace, there are plenty of ways to impact your reputation outside of the workplace.

When it comes to building your great reputation at work, do what it takes to hit the ground running. Take it one step at a time, and don't be afraid if you stumble now and then. After all, if good things really *don't* come to those who wait, then imagine what's in store for you by jumping in with two feet and making the most of your new experience.

From effectively introducing yourself around the office, to looking the part so that people focus on you, and not your wardrobe, building your reputation always boils down to the choices you make. Use this guide to make the right choices, so you get off to a great career.

UNSPOKEN RULE #2

Your Fork Is Not a Shovel,
Your Knife Is Not a Saw

**Dazzle Them at Business Lunches, Dinners, and Anyplace
Else Where a Fork Is Required**

Inside This Chapter:

Learn What It Takes to Outclass the Competition

- **Step #1**: Give Yourself the Clue Nobody Else Will
- **Step #2**: Remember, It's Not about the Food
- **Step #3**: Master the Art of Conversation
- **Step #4**: Follow the 80/20 Rule of Dining Etiquette
- **Step #5**: Develop Etiquette Confidence for Any Situation

Introduction:
The Big Picture behind Business Etiquette

Think that a knife and fork are just sweet, innocent dining utensils? Think again.

Consider the story of John, a hardworking nice guy, who happened to be an intern at one of the world's largest consulting firms between his junior and senior years in college. Like many interns who went before him, John was eager to impress and tried like heck to do so, with the hopes that he would land a juicy full-time job offer upon successful completion of his internship. John gave his best effort on all of his projects, got along well with his boss, and even joined the company softball team for the summer. Things were going along smashingly for John and the full-time offer seemed like a done deal.

And then, suddenly, things went wrong . . . very, very wrong.

It all started the night of the annual company dinner, held at the end of each summer to thank all of the interns for their hard work on behalf of the firm. The company pulls out all of the stops for this event: a 12-piece band, plenty of hors d'oeuvres, and a five-course meal to boot. Many of the firm's partners attended the event, where the majority were meeting the interns for the very first time. Sitting at a table surrounded by bigwigs, dining on a salad and soufflé, John felt like he had the world at his fingertips. He could almost smell that full-time job offer . . . not to mention the roast beef, which he dug into with abandon.

And, friends, that's where the trouble really started. To begin with, let's just say that John didn't have the world's greatest table manners. Sure, we've all seen worse, but you have to wonder why a smart, polished intern would hold a knife and fork like a little kid, or eat a piece of beef with such enthusiasm that you'd think he had hunted down the animal and brought it to the table himself.

Had John's behavior ended there, perhaps we could forget that the whole evening had ever happened and move on. Except that John decided to talk. After all, it wasn't every day that a lowly intern got to dine with a big-deal senior partner at a swanky company event, and John wasn't going to waste this opportunity. And so, he talked. And talked. And talked. You see, like some of us, John tends to become overly chatty when he gets nervous, and nervous he was. So he rambled and asked questions like "Are you married?" to one of the female partners sitting at the table, not knowing that she had just gotten divorced. Oops.

What NOT to Say at Work

- *"When are you due?"* Even if she looks like she's going to give birth tomorrow, do not ask this one. Trust me, it can really backfire. All it takes is asking this question one time to someone who is *not* pregnant for you to never want to ask again.

- *"Isn't George Bush the best?"* Unless you are at a Republican convention, avoid this one—and all politics for that matter. Sure, you're allowed to have opinions about politics, religion, sex, or other issues of the day—but keep them to yourself at work.

- *"How's your husband?" Reply:* "We're getting divorced, thank you very much." The moral of the story? Tread carefully when it comes to asking questions about family. You may disagree with this one—after all, we all love talking about family, right? Sure, people love talking about their kids . . . except about the one who has been in drug rehab four times. Until you know someone beyond a first introduction or two, best to steer clear of too many questions on family, personal relationships, kids, and health.

- *"How much did your house cost?"* People have funny ways of trying to find out how much money you have, and this question is just one example. Avoid the money stuff at all costs—pardon the pun.

At the End of the Day, Do Manners Really Matter?

Is it a crime to have iffy table manners? Is it so wrong to ask a personal question or two at a social function for work? After all, isn't performance what really counts? The short answer is, it depends. As we read in the last chapter, if you're the next Warren Buffett or Oprah Winfrey, for instance, you can probably get away with all kinds of stuff when it comes to corporate etiquette, including bad manners at the dinner table, and nobody will bat an eye.

But for most of us, it's another story. For instance, imagine that you've been invited to interview for a job with a new company and you're being taken out to lunch by the recruiter and hiring manager. As you sit across the table from two people who aren't necessarily aware of how great and capable and talented you are, first impressions are everything. If your dining savvy isn't up to snuff—whether it's knowing what to order, how to eat it, or what to say during that meal—rest assured, it will matter, because they don't know you yet. Until they do, don't assume that they will give you the benefit of the doubt. Sure, they may overlook the fact that you don't know how to properly hold a knife and a fork because they think you've got a great résumé or seem terrific. On the other hand, they might wonder if you are who you really say you are. After all, it sends a slightly mixed message to talk about your professionalism while you're chewing with your mouth open, don't you think?

Who Picks Up the Check?

Remember, he who does the asking does the paying when it comes to dining out on the job—this goes for men and women. If you're ever asked out to lunch for a job interview or by the boss, or anything else that is work-related, don't worry about picking up the check—if they asked you, they should be the ones to pay the bill. However, note that even if you do the asking, the more senior person at the table will usually pick up the check, regardless. So if you happen to mention to your boss, *"I'd love to schedule some time to discuss the project further with you. Would you be free for lunch?"* you can still safely assume that the boss is paying.

When do YOU pay? Use your best judgment here. Assume that if you're doing the asking, you're doing the paying. If you are dining out with peers at a friendly, informal lunch, chances are that you will all split the check. And remember, if you're taking out a client, the client doesn't pay. Don't worry about going broke: If your meals are for legitimate business purposes and you've gotten the appropriate approvals, chances are that you aren't personally paying for it anyway—so you can thank your company for that.

Also consider that business etiquette in social situations is one of the many ways in which you are evaluated as an employee, too. Like it or not, your boss may question whether he can put you in front of a potential client, or even in front of his own boss, depending on how well you make chitchat and how you hold your fork. The bottom line is that bad table manners leave a bad impression and simply don't reinforce the professional, polished, confident image that we all want to convey when it comes to our careers.

When It Comes to Corporate Etiquette, It's Time to Sweat the Small Stuff

In John's case, manners really did matter, because he didn't wind up getting an offer with the company at the end of the summer. Can we say it's because of his blunders during that annual dinner? Nobody will know for sure, but consider the fact that John had committed some fairly bad no-nos in front of some senior people, most of whom had only met John for the first time that night.

You see, they hadn't seen all of the hard work and contributions he had made over the summer and didn't know that John had the potential to be a real asset to the company. Instead, they saw someone who embarrassed himself and, as a result, the organization. After all, this was a consulting firm:

They didn't make products—they sold business solutions, innovative ideas, and knowledge capital. Like many professional services firms, from law to accounting to advertising, the employees *were* the product, and everything they did and said was a very real reflection of the firm and its brand. Plus, with so many interns and only a limited number of full-time offers, it was easy to disqualify John over his lack of business savvy, poor table manners, or anything else that didn't measure up.

Can it be said that a knife and fork brought down one intern's career? Possibly so. But perhaps the message behind this cautionary tale, and inside this very book, is this: Whoever said "Don't sweat the small stuff" was wrong. Dead wrong.

Does it really matter how you eat with a fork? You bet it does. Because when you get the small stuff right, the big stuff—your job, your career, and your success—gets a lot easier.

Step #1:
Give Yourself the Clue Nobody Else Will

After attending many a business lunch, corporate event, dinner outing, and more under the guise of "work fun" (raise your hand if you think that's an oxymoron), I feel compelled to write the following rather obvious statement: Your fork is not a shovel. And while we're on the subject, I might also mention that your knife is not a saw and that your napkin should not be waved around like you're heading off to a bullfight later on today.

Naturally, you already know this, and plenty more. Chew with your mouth open? Certainly not! But here's the thing: We all think we have great table manners. We all think the gross, clueless dining companion is somebody else. But when was the last time you saw yourself eating? Like many things that fall under the corporate etiquette umbrella, we're often the last ones to know when there's a problem. Can you honestly imagine your boss saying "Listen, you've been doing great work, but you've really got to stop chewing with your mouth open. It's grossing everybody out." If the boss is like most of us, he'd do just about anything to avoid breaking the bad news to you.

When it comes to some of the more delicate areas of business savvy, including dining etiquette, you've got to give yourself the clue nobody else will give you. Remember, dining out isn't just about dining out—it's another opportunity to build up your reputation . . . or kick it down a notch or two. Why risk hurting your professional image over something as dumb as a fork?

As we enter a world of office picnics, lunches with the boss, and various other outings at work, allow me to share a few of the fine points (and really obvious ones, too) about fine dining and everything else that comes with socializing on the job. Some of the points discussed below may seem silly, overly detailed, or simply unnecessary, but think of dining etiquette like pieces in a puzzle, and you need all of the little pieces to get the right outcome.

For all of you well-mannered, elegant readers out there, feel free to drop this book anonymously on the desk of that oaf sitting next to you. For everyone else, read on.

Step #2:
Remember, It's Not about the Food

You're sitting at work when the phone rings. It's your boss, who mentions that Mr. Bigwig Client happens to be in town for the day, and you'll be taking him out to lunch, along with your boss, to Chez Henri in 30 minutes. If this is your first real business lunch, you may be a tad nervous, or simply wonder exactly what to do, say, or wear. Don't panic: When this is over, you're going to be as smooth as Miss Manners.

What to Wear to a Business Event

You never know when your boss is going to invite you out to lunch at the Four Seasons, so make sure you look sharp, no matter what the occasion. If you are being invited out to lunch, don't be afraid to call the restaurant ahead of time and ask if there is a dress code—some restaurants still do require jackets for men, for example. In most situations, if you're already dressed for work, you will probably be dressed appropriately for whatever lunch or event you've got scheduled, assuming you follow the guidelines we outlined earlier and don't work for a company where anything goes.

When does it pay to get gussied up for a business event? For plenty of situations, particularly if your company holds a formal gala, awards banquet, or other type of formal social event. In those cases, formal attire (think tuxedo, not suit) may be appropriate. If you're taking a client out to lunch or visiting him at his or her workplace, it wouldn't be unusual to wear a suit. The best rule of thumb? Let the event guide you and use common sense: If you're wearing a suit to the company picnic or flip-flops to the Four Seasons, you know you're in trouble!

If there is one unspoken rule to remember when you're out at a business lunch, social event, or anything else work-related, it's that it is never about the food. It's not about the fact that you can order whatever you want (you can't, by the way, but more on that later) because the company is paying for it, or because you've never eaten at Chez Henri before and you can't wait to try the escargot. Whether you're dining out to entertain a client or to get to know your boss, socializing at work always boils down to one key idea: building trust. Ultimately, you are there to deepen a connection, further a relationship, and strengthen ties, so if the restaurant forgot to put your salad dressing on the side, you can live with it.

Step #3:
Master the Art of Conversation

So, how do you build trust and relationships in business social settings? Master the art of conversation. At the very least, force yourself to ask good questions and talk about something besides the weather. Whether you're at a cocktail function or formal business dinner, knowing how to communicate with people at all levels of the company is critical.

Dos and Don'ts
for Becoming a Great Conversationalist

DON'T *FORGET TO INTRODUCE YOURSELF!* This basic step is often overlooked at dining functions. When you arrive at the table, before you sit down, take a moment to make sure that everyone knows who you are. When the moment presents itself, extend your hand, smile, look someone in the eye, and simply say something along the lines of "Hi, I'm Alice Smith. I work with John in Accounting. So nice to meet you." While it is the host's job to make sure that everyone at the table has been properly introduced, there is nothing wrong with helping the process along in case that hasn't happened. Introduce the person on your left to the person on your right, and so on. If you really want to get technical, keep in mind that a younger person is always introduced to the more senior person: "Mr. Bigshot, may I present Younger Intern?"

DON'T *BE AFRAID TO TAKE A RISK OR TWO,* suggests Keith Ferrazzi, co-author of *Never Eat Alone: And Other Secrets to Success, One Relationship at a Time.* This doesn't mean that you dump the details of the latest fight with your boyfriend on your dining companions, but don't be afraid to show your human, real side if you really want to create connections. If that means sharing with your boss "I'm nervous about our big sales meeting next week. I know you've been through a dozen of these—can you offer any suggestions?" then don't hold back.

DON'T *BE OVERCOME WITH A CASE OF SHYNESS.* When it comes to asking questions, to sharing ideas, to exchanging information, you simply cannot shrink and hide in a corner. Force yourself to talk if you must, but do it. If you really freeze in these types of situations, have a few talking points prepared ahead of time. Do some homework before your event so that you can dazzle your dinner companions with the latest information about your clients or a new product.

DON'T *INTERRUPT.* Even if you don't intend to come across as rude, you send the message that "my idea is way more important than yours" when you do. Sometimes I have to literally press my lips together to keep from interrupting (scary, but true), and I know others who do, in fact, bite their tongues to keep their mouths shut. If you tend to be on the chatty side, think about employing your own technique to keep the lips zipped.

DON'T *RAMBLE OR DOMINATE THE CONVERSATION.* Like the interrupter, the rambler sends the unintentional message of "Listen to me, everybody!" This may be a sign of insecurity, immaturity, nervousness, or someone who loves being the center of attention, which are definitely not messages you or I want to send. At the very least, it comes across as unprofessional and annoying. If you feel like you're doing all the talking, STOP. Say, "Gee, I feel like I'm doing all the talking! Let me stop myself and have you tell me what's been going on with your latest project."

DO *LISTEN.* So often, we only half-listen to someone else, and while they are talking, we are crafting our own witty comeback to offer once they are done. Or we pretend we are listening by nodding and smiling, but meanwhile, we're thinking, "I wonder if I'll have time to go to the gym after work." Instead, force yourself to truly focus on the people you are dining with. Use good eye contact, smile, and show them you are really with them by asking good questions that refer to what they just said: "When you said that sales were down, were you referring to our team or to the entire department?"

DO *THINK OF A CONVERSATION LIKE A GOOD TENNIS MATCH,* and your job is to keep the ball in play. Break the ice by asking interesting, open-ended questions, like "What did you think of today's announcement on CNBC?" or "What good conferences or seminars have you attended this year?" If you are the youngest person at the table, or you're surrounded by people who are more senior in title than you, you may feel strange initiating conversation with Mr. Bigwig or even with your boss. Let them serve the ball first, and once they do, don't be afraid to return the serve with some intelligent comments.

DO *KEEP THE CONVERSATION FOCUSED ON THE LIGHTER SIDE OF THINGS,* particularly early into a business meal. Many etiquette guides will tell you to hold off on the business stuff until you're sipping coffee and having some dessert. In today's busy workplace, people can't afford to linger too long over lunch, so let your host set the pace for when the serious talk should begin.

Get the Conversation Ball Rolling

Cat got your tongue? Not sure what to say to a stranger? There are tons of icebreaker questions out there—here are a few to try:

The "Decide" Questions: "What made you decide to . . ."

- ". . . work for this company?"
- ". . . come to this event?"
- ". . . go to Boston University?"

The "Have you/Can you" Questions:

- "Have you been to any good conferences or seminars lately?"
- "Can you recommend any good books on time management?"
- "What good things have you heard about our speaker tonight?"

The "What is" Questions:

- "What is your approach to time management?"
- "What is the most interesting project you've been working on lately?"
- "What suggestions do you have for someone who is new to the company?"
- "What was your first job?"

Step #4:
Follow the 80/20 Rule of Dining Etiquette

When it comes to learning the art and science of fine dining, you could read volumes on the topic and still not be done by the time you retire. Sure, you can become an expert in knives and forks, or you can adopt this dining version of the Pareto Principle to learn a few key points that will work wonders for you. The Pareto Principle is a mathematical formula created by Italian economist Vilfredo Pareto in 1906 to describe how 80 percent of the wealth in Italy was held by 20 percent of the people at that time. Today, this concept is often used in business settings: For instance, a company might note that 80 percent of its sales come from 20 percent of its customers, and so on.

What does this mean to you? Adopt the 80/20 rule when it comes to dining etiquette. Rather than worry about every little detail and knowing all the rules, focus on the key few that will give you the most bang for your buck. Whether you're dining with the boss or the boss's daughter, you'll do fine if you follow the points below.

Point #1: To drink out of the right water glass, think BMW
Here's an easy way to avoid drinking out of your boss's water glass: Think BMW. As you look down at your place setting and scan your eyes left to right, think **b**read, **m**iddle, **w**ater. The bread plate will always be to your left, and your water glass (and other liquids) will always be to your right.

Point #2: Keep your napkin in your lap
Here's a question that has caused many a sleepless night: When should I put my napkin in my lap? Answer: the minute everyone has sat down. Generally, your dining napkin is placed on your lap and folded in half. Please, don't spread it across your lap like you're getting ready to have a picnic on it, and for the love of God, don't tuck it into a shirt, a belt, or anyplace else.

Throughout your meal, your napkin stays in your lap. If you need to leave the table, place your napkin in your chair while you are gone. Please, don't put your gross, ketchup-stained napkin on the table for the rest of us to look at. (In fact, the word "ketchup" shouldn't even come across your lips during a fine dining experience.) And while we're on the subject of gross, if you're even thinking of blowing your nose in your napkin, please don't dine with me, or anyone else who wishes to have an appetite while dining. Ick.

Point #3: Your fork is not a shovel
It's not a magic wand, a spear, or something to click against your teeth. It's also not something to be clenched with a fist, like a little kid holding on to a toy for dear life. As silly as it sounds, many of us don't hold our dining utensils correctly or even come close. While there are a few different ways to hold and use a knife and fork correctly, the most common method used in the United States is as follows:

- When you eat, your fork is held in your right hand, like a pencil. (For all of you lefties out there, the fork is still held in the right hand.)

- When you cut your food, switch hands. Fork goes in the left hand, knife goes in the right to cut. Using your index finger, point your fork with tines facing down to pierce your food. By the way, don't cut up all of your food at once! Unless you're Mommy cutting up steak for little Junior, this kind of stuff is for kids only.

- Switch the fork back into the right hand to eat . . . and presto! Elegant dining!

Point #4: Keep your order simple
When it comes to ordering food, remember one thing: Preserve your dignity. That means spaghetti and lobster are out, and so is anything that requires the use of fingers. No gnawing on a chicken bone or grabbing a slice of pizza with your hands. While you're at it, avoid foods that seem

complicated, like fajitas (too labor intensive) or certain kinds of fish (too many bones to pick out). Instead, stick to simple, safe food and save the exotic entrées for another time.

Don't Go Overboard with Ordering!

Should you order an appetizer? What about alcohol? Check out our ordering tips here.

- *Remember, there is an order to ordering.* When you sit down, don't immediately start reading the menu—wait for your host to do so first. When it comes to ordering, a gracious host will usually defer to the guests and let them go first, or the server will decide (usually by starting with the women at the table).

- *Take cues from your host about how much to order.* If your host says, "I hear the shrimp cocktail is great here," or "You must try the cheesecake," then you know that you're safe to order an appetizer or dessert. If you're just not sure if it's OK to order a soup or salad, or anything else, don't be afraid to politely ask: "John, will you be having soup?"

- *Price-wise,* don't order the most expensive thing on the menu, but don't feel like you have to order the least expensive item, either. Middle of the road is fine.

- *If you've got food allergies* or other personal reasons for not eating certain food, or simply hate something you're being served, the key here is to be gracious. If you're able to let your server know discreetly that you can't eat something, then go ahead. Otherwise, be polite, never criticize what you are being served, make an attempt to take a taste or two, and move on. If it's not the greatest meal of your life, let it go. Remember, you're not there for the food, you're there for your job, your career, and your success.

- *To drink or not to drink:* That is the question! Don't order alcohol unless your host does, and even then, tread very carefully. While there is nothing wrong with slowly sipping a glass of wine at a business dinner, you need to know your limits and watch yourself. In fact, if you really want to stay sharp and sound professional, it may be best to avoid drinking altogether. For some of us, all it takes is one extra drink to get the dumb comments started, so why take a chance?

- *Even if you're out with the VP* who is downing tequila shots like there is no tomorrow and egging you on to do the same, resist the urge to party. It may seem fine, even more than fine, to go crazy with the rest of them, but think twice. As fun and social an event as it may seem, it's still a work event at the end of the day and people will remember what you did and said long after they've recovered from their hangovers.

- *If you're under 21,* don't even think about alcohol at anything work-related. Even if it's an open bar and you're convinced nobody is watching or would even care, don't do it. Trust me, many an intern has been undone by an open bar at a company cocktail hour. Don't be one of them!

Step #5:
Develop Etiquette Confidence for Any Situation

Now that you know the rules—spoken and unspoken—about the art and science of socializing on the job, it's up to you to apply them. But be warned: Just when you think you've got something on Miss Manners, life throws you a curveball, and the next thing you know, you're stuck at a networking event where you know no one and have been dragged into a really, really boring conversation with somebody who you're dying to get away from. Now what?

If you've found yourself in a tricky social situation, fear not. Chances are that if you're polite, friendly, and professional, you'll be able to handle nearly anything. But in case you find yourself needing to make small talk with Attila the Hun, try a few of these strategies on to handle the tough times.

Tricky Situation #1: Help! I'm at a cocktail party for work and know absolutely nobody
Try this: Do your homework ahead of time. Study up on five or six people attending the event whom you really want to know, and then make it your mission to meet them during the networking event. When you approach them, you'll already have a few things to discuss based on your research. (Note: Best to keep this strategy to yourself. There is a fine line between doing homework and stalking, and some people may get a tad nervous to discover that you know more about them than they do.)

Tricky Situation #2: Help! I'm at a cocktail party for work and everybody already seems to be involved in a conversation. Should I interrupt to try to meet someone?

Try this: If you arrive at an event and everyone seems to have found their friends already, don't feel shut out. Instead, approach a group that looks friendly or try to find people with whom you might have something in common. Don't interrupt anyone, but do introduce yourself when you sense a break in conversation: "Hi, I didn't want to interrupt, but I just wanted to introduce myself. I'm Alice Smith, from Accounting. A couple of you look familiar to me—didn't I see you at last month's networking event?" If a group feels too intimidating, strike up a conversation with someone at the buffet or bar instead when the timing is right. Whatever you do, don't stand around all night in a corner talking to the same one or two folks. Force yourself to break out and introduce yourself to others—don't expect others to come to you.

Tricky Situation #3: Help! I'm trapped in a conversation with someone who is incredibly boring! How can I get away without seeming like a jerk?
Try this: "John, I don't want to interrupt you, but I do need to catch Jan before she heads out this evening. Please excuse me." Or: "John, it's been great to chat, but I want to make sure I have time to meet a couple of clients that are here. I hope our paths cross again." Another approach: Involve others in your conversation: "Alice, have you met John in Accounting?" Just because John bores you to tears doesn't mean he drives Alice nuts. Whatever you say, be friendly and courteous, and just make sure you can back it up. If you tell John that you need to end your conversation to make a phone call, and then he sees you chatting with friends by the bar, he'll know soon enough that the phone call was just an excuse to get away from him.

Tricky Situation #4: Help! My boss is drunk!
Try this: If you're out with people who wind up getting

intoxicated, whether it's coworkers, clients, or even your boss, don't panic, don't judge, and don't tell everyone at work the next day about what a bunch of drunkards you were out with. In this type of situation, your best move is to make sure that nobody is in a position to harm themselves or others, so offer to serve as the designated driver or call someone a cab. Then go home, before you're tempted to join them.

Tricky Situation #5: Help! My cell phone just rang during lunch with my boss!
Try this: Turn it off! After all, cell phones have no place at a business lunch, dinner, or other business social setting—and that goes for BlackBerrys or other PDAs, too. Even if your boss is chatting away on his cell phone during lunch (which is rude, rude, rude), don't you do it, too. If your phone does ring, simply turn it off quickly and apologize. If you ab-solutely must take a call, let your boss know ahead of time by saying something like: "John, my mother might be calling me on my cell phone during lunch to give me a quick up-date on my dad's operation." If and when the phone rings, quickly leave the table and take the call (briefly!) outside the restaurant to avoid disturbing others.

Whether you're attending your first business social event or your twentieth, the moral of the story is always the same: You're not there for the food or the open bar—you're there to build relationships. A business lunch or office barbecue is a terrific place for others to get to know you, learn to trust you, and give your career a little boost. Keep the focus off your table manners, so that others can focus on you instead.

UNSPOKEN RULE #3

The Workplace Meeting Is Your Career's Secret Weapon

Leverage This Opportunity to Showcase Your Strengths to an Audience

Introduction:
Workplace Meetings—
Much More than Meets the Eye

A workplace ritual often characterized as more boring than watching paint dry and more painful than hearing a thousand fingernails dragged across a blackboard, the meeting gets a bad rap by many employees. Instead, we take a different approach to the business meeting, which, when done right, can be the new professional's best friend.

However, if the meeting is to become a friend instead of a foe, it's important to adopt a change in mind-set. For example, when you hear the word "meeting" in the context of work, what usually pops into your head? If you're like most of us, you've probably conjured up some image of a stuffy, dimly lit room filled with bored-looking people watching an even more boring PowerPoint presentation being delivered by the most boring person on the planet. And who could blame you? Most of us have sat through boring, unproductive, uninspiring meetings, and we come to associate them with a version of workplace hell. Entirely understandable.

But meetings go way beyond this scenario—in fact, meetings are happening in your workplace all the time, at practically every moment, often without you even realizing it. If you look up the word "meeting" in the dictionary or on the Internet, you'll find plenty of definitions and meanings for the word. For example, *Merriam-Webster's Collegiate*

Dictionary defines a meeting as a "formally arranged gathering," which is the definition that you and I usually associate with the word. But meetings are also defined as "small, informal gatherings" or even "a casual or unexpected convergence."

Does this mean that chatting around the water cooler is a meeting? Or that when you bump into a couple of sales reps in the company cafeteria, you're actually having a meeting? In a manner of speaking, that's exactly what we are saying. "The marketing team is meeting in conference room A at 10:00 am on Wednesday" is one version of a meeting, but there are many other ways that we encounter our work colleagues to share ideas, exchange information, and persuade others to a point of view—formally and otherwise. Our goal is to understand when these opportunities present themselves and how to take advantage of them in a way that strengthens relationships, showcases our skills and expertise, and, in small and big ways, can further our career. This doesn't mean that every conversation is a mini-meeting, or that every meeting is an opportunity for you to take over and act like the CEO. But it does mean that when done right, over the long term, the meeting can help bump you up a notch or two.

Step #1:
Understand the Mystery of Meetings— and How to Crack the Code

If you've been working for any amount of time, it's pretty likely that you've attended a meeting or two—perhaps dozens. Whether the meeting involved two people or twenty, chances are you were told to show up somewhere, at some time, and, well . . . the rest is just going to be a surprise.

Think I'm kidding? The truth is that most of us are told very little about the meetings we're expected to attend. If you're lucky, maybe you were given an agenda ahead of time, or, even better, you were actually told what the goals or objectives and desired outcomes were for that meeting. Best of all, maybe you were told what your specific contributions would be—in other words, you were given an explanation as to why you were being asked to attend that particular meeting. But more often than not, we're left in the dark when it comes to the specifics of what will happen when meeting time rolls around—beyond "We're going to talk about our goals for next quarter."

The Problem with Mystery

What's the big deal? you ask. So what if you don't know every little detail about an upcoming meeting? Sometimes, there is nothing wrong with an impromptu, spontaneous meeting—it may be necessary, particularly if some pressing issue or urgent matter has come up at work that requires immediate attention and action.

Meetings dealing with work emergencies aside, several problems arise when you simply show up to a meeting without knowing much beyond whether or not breakfast will be served. Here are some examples of these potential problems:

- *YOUR TIME IS WASTED.* When a meeting lacks an agenda, a clear focus, or a specific start and end time, and has no clear goals, objectives, or outcomes, chances are that it simply won't be a productive use of your time. True, you may have no choice in whether or not to attend, but it's never fun sitting in a chair knowing that the clock is ticking away when you've got a million things to do.

- *YOU MIGHT BE CAUGHT OFF GUARD.* Surprise! You walk into your meeting and discover that your boss's boss has decided to make an impromptu appearance. And guess what? He'd like an update from you on Client X and Client Y—*now*. Sure, you might be able to pull off something . . . or maybe you're totally unprepared.

- *YOU DON'T KNOW THE FULL STORY.* Sometimes, a meeting can resemble the workplace equivalent of *Dallas*. Instead of innocently joining a group of colleagues in a conference room, you're really walking into the living room of the world's most dysfunctional family. In other words, if you're not prepared in advance, there may be all kinds of office politics going on in that meeting room, and you don't want to say or do the wrong thing and step into a minefield.

- *YOU DON'T APPEAR AS SHARP AND SMART AS YOU REALLY ARE.* Walking into a meeting with no clue what's about to happen is sort of like taking a pop quiz. You may get lucky and do just fine, or maybe you're like most of us: If you had just a little time to review your notes or study in advance, you'd definitely get the A. When you walk into a room prepared, polished, and ready to go, it's like studying in advance for a test—you know what you're doing, and it shows. When you show up and plan to "wing it," you're taking a risk that may not land you the A in the workplace.

When You're Not Running the Show

Just when you thought I couldn't possibly have anything else
to complain about when it comes to meetings, I have one
more issue: We're not in charge! Call me a control freak (or
incredibly arrogant, I suppose), but I often think that meetings I attend would be much, much less painful—or at least
shorter—if *I* was the one running them. Feel the same way?
Many of us do, and that's probably because meetings force
us to be at the mercy of someone else, and that "someone
else" could be the world's worst meeting facilitator. After all,
we aren't the ones showing up with no agenda, no plan, and
no time frame. Someone else is.

It's easy to blame our bosses, coworkers, or everyone else
on the planet for why meetings stink. But we're not helpless
victims. Whether you're the one in charge of the meeting or
not, there is no excuse for not showing up as well prepared
as you can be. There is always a way to get the information
you need—the key is knowing where to look.

Your Job? Crack the Meeting Mystery Code!

Don't get caught with your pants down when it comes to
meetings. It's easy to be prepared, and when you are, you
ooze confidence and professionalism. You show people what
you are really capable of, and even better, you might surprise
them by pulling a few tricks out of your hat. But in order to
dazzle them, you need to be one step ahead of them.

Getting Information—the Party-Planning Approach

Imagine you've been invited to attend a party. In order to
make the most of your upcoming soiree, you might ask a

few questions of the host ahead of time: *"Who else will be there?" "What are you wearing?" "Is there anything that I can bring?"* Believe it or not, prepping for your next meeting isn't too different.

When you think about your next meeting, imagine you're being invited to a party and ask a few questions first.

WHO ELSE WILL BE THERE? You may not need to ask this question before a meeting, but if you're not sure who will be in attendance, find out. Take the time to email your boss or whoever is planning the meeting and simply ask the question. As we stated earlier, you don't want to be surprised or caught off guard if Mr. Bigshot decides to attend your meeting that week. Equally important, meetings are excellent opportunities to connect with new colleagues and network with people with whom you might otherwise not come into contact. For instance, when you know the "guest list" ahead of time, you can use the meeting as a reason to connect further. For example, why not drop an email before the meeting to someone you'd like to get to know? You could write something like "Melissa, I notice that you'll be attending Mark's meeting next week. If you have some time, I'd love to catch up with you afterward and learn a little more about what is going on in your department."

WHAT ARE YOU WEARING? What does a dress code really reveal about a party? Well, if you're expected to show up in a tuxedo, you're probably expecting champagne and caviar, not beer and Cheetos. The same is true at work—and dress often reflects the tone and level of formality at any given meeting.

When it comes to this question, don't miss the message: Even if you know exactly what to wear, the real issue is, what kind of meeting is this, really? Is the tone light, informal, fun? Do people interrupt one another or shout out ideas as they pop up? Is this the kind of meeting where anyone can contribute, or does the boss do most of the talking? Once you figure out the tone of the meeting, you'll have a much better sense of how to act and what to say (or not say).

WHAT CAN I BRING? When you ask this of your host, you're really asking "How can I contribute? How can I help?" Even if your host says "You don't need to bring anything," don't believe him. Bring stuff to a meeting. For example, if you know that your boss is planning to discuss last quarter's sales results, why not take the initiative to bring copies of data or spreadsheets that he might want to refer to with the group? During a meeting, questions come up, people need answers, and you look like the hero when you give them the facts they need at their fingertips.

Step #2:
You've Done Your Homework, Now Dazzle Them

Once you've done your homework, don't put all that effort to waste. Make sure that you really know how to put your best foot forward at your next meeting.

Dos and Don'ts:
Top Tips for Making Meetings Work for You

DO *SHOW UP EARLY.* If you really want to make a splash, show up early (not just "on time") to your next meeting. Even if nobody else does, do it anyway. At the very least, you'll stand out (in a good way), and the effort shows that you respect other people's time. Plus, showing up a few minutes ahead of time gives you a chance to meet and network with coworkers who may also have arrived ahead of schedule.

DO *LISTEN.* Even if you've been given a specific role to play at a meeting, you should spend the majority of your time actively listening and observing, not speaking. The meeting is your chance to learn, so pretend you're in school: Listen, take notes, and get as much information as you can.

DO *BE PROACTIVE AND BRING EXTRA INFORMA-TION,* data, or materials that you think will help illustrate a particular point or idea during the meeting. Most of us simply show up to a meeting with a pad of paper, sit back, and let other people do the work. Bring something to the meeting table by anticipating what is most needed by your boss and coworkers.

DO *HAVE SOMETHING TO CONTRIBUTE.* Here is where things get tricky: You annoy people if you say too much . . . but you may not impress them if you say nothing at all. Unless you're at a very large meeting where everyone is mostly listening, it isn't out of line for you to offer a point or two. Your comments should be short, sweet, and to the point—but remember, you were invited for a reason, so don't be afraid to speak up. David Roberts, president and CEO of Equity Methods, recalls that when he was employed by a large consulting firm, a "20-minute rule" was used to informally keep consultants on track. "If 20 minutes went by and you hadn't yet spoken, you probably shouldn't be at that meeting," he explained. The moral of the story? Force yourself to speak up and add value at every meeting you attend.

DO *ADDRESS YOUR COMMENTS TO EVERYONE.* Meetings are a group activity, so when you do speak, use a clear voice and make eye contact with the group. If you've got absolutely no idea about what to say to the group, consider asking an intelligent, well-thought-out question or two.

DO *FOLLOW UP.* Email participants after a meeting to further discuss a point, or touch base with your boss's colleague to provide the information you agreed to supply during the meeting. Even something as simple as an email that reads "John, I thought you might be interested in that article I mentioned during our meeting—here is a copy for you" goes a long way to show that you're thinking long after the meeting is over. Plus, if you didn't have a chance to say or do much during the meeting, follow-up is always a meaningful way to make an impact on others.

DO *TAKE ADVANTAGE OF MEETINGS* to showcase or highlight your other talents and abilities. People may be familiar with your ability to do your daily tasks, so use the meeting as a chance to demonstrate something new or different that you can also do, but may not have the chance to do at work, like your terrific public-speaking abilities.

DO *ASK FOR A JOB TO DO.* If you'd like to be guaranteed a little visibility at a meeting, particularly if you're shy or simply not comfortable speaking up in a group setting, ask your meeting host for something specific to do, whether it's sharing a specific agenda item, taking notes, arranging the computer equipment, etc.

DON'T *ARRIVE EMPTY-HANDED.* Always bring a pen and a leather portfolio (or a pad of paper). This seems incredibly obvious, yet people will arrive at meetings, seminars, even conferences without anything to write with, let alone a business card or two. It should go without saying, but showing up empty-handed to a meeting sends a clear message to others that you couldn't be bothered with being prepared.

DON'T *POOH-POOH EVERYTHING.* Nobody likes the person who shows up to a meeting and only offers reasons why things won't work. If someone has an idea or concept that you think is harebrained, try to see the merit in the idea. Disagree respectfully if you must, but always offer solutions or alternate ideas instead. Be positive, upbeat, and keep the negative comments to a minimum.

DON'T *TAKE MEETINGS FOR GRANTED.* Many of us have the same kinds of meetings on a regular basis with the same people, and it's easy to let things slide when that happens. After all, if you've got a staff meeting every Monday morning, will anyone really notice or care if you come in a couple of minutes late every once in a while? The answer is yes and yes—actions always speak louder than words. Even if your meetings are a routine part of your work week, don't slack or get lazy when it comes to preparing and showing up professionally for them.

And the DON'T of all meeting DON'Ts . . .

DON'T *PONTIFICATE, ELABORATE, OR OTHERWISE DOMINATE THE CONVERSATION.* Take this one to heart: If you're low on the totem pole at work or otherwise the new kid on the block, keep your comments to a minimum. If you're asked a question, by all means, answer, but answer succinctly. When you're new to the workplace game, adding more than your two cents will really, really rub your coworkers the wrong way. You've been warned!

Step #3:
Attend Meetings—
Even If You Don't Have Any to Attend

Until now, we've assumed that you attend meetings on a regular basis. But what if this isn't the case? In many work environments, employees spend hours alone, inside a cubicle—and meetings may not happen much at all. In a busy work environment, conference calls, Webinars, and even emails have replaced meetings and other face-to-face interactions in many instances. Additionally, because of budgetary or other policy reasons, newer professionals may find themselves left off the guest list when it comes to attending meetings, particularly for the off-site, more prestigious ones.

If you aren't attending many meetings, you can change that situation, and it's easier than you might think. In fact, if you haven't attended a meeting in a few months, you *should* try to change that. After all, it's tough to get known around the office for your insight, professionalism, or great ideas when you're buried inside your cubicle all day.

Why bother trying to attend meetings that you don't actually have to attend? Isn't this a waste of time? Hardly. Remember—when done right, meetings are a unique way to learn and boost your profile and career.

So, what does it take to get a seat at the meeting table? Try out a few ideas:

- Invite yourself to a meeting. For example, let's imagine that you run into a couple of casual acquaintances from the Sales Department while you're pouring your morning coffee. Say something like "Listen, the next time your team is meeting to discuss the upcoming product launch, would you mind if I sat in to learn a little more? Our department is working on the marketing end of the launch and it would be helpful to hear about things from your perspective." "Bump into" people on purpose and use this technique again and again.

- Offer to be a volunteer at an upcoming meeting or conference. If you've been left off the invitation list for a meeting or an event and you'd like to attend, see if you can help out in some way to attend part or all of the event. Offer to be a people mover to help attendees find their rooms, or help with setting up the speaker's laptop computer, making the PowerPoint slides, or anything else you can think of that hasn't already been assigned.

- Let your boss know that you'd like to attend more meetings. This is an easy step to skip, because many of us assume that our boss already knows what we want. This may not be the case, so be very clear about what you'd like, and then ask for it, graciously. You might ask, "Paul, the next time you and Bob are meeting about such-and-such, I'd really like to sit in. Would that be possible?" Or: "Paul, I know that you are putting together a list of possible attendees for the annual research conference. I'd like to be considered for the following reasons . . ."

ONE NOTE WHEN IT COMES TO GETTING INVITED: Being proactive is great, but don't push yourself on anyone. If you notice that nobody else on your team or at your level in the organization is getting invited to certain meetings, then consider this a sign that you probably shouldn't be at these meetings, either.

Step #4:
Understand Why You're Not Getting Invited to Meetings (and Other Tricky Situations)

If you find yourself repeatedly left out of meetings, events, conferences, or other workplace gatherings, there may be a reason why. Consider the following reasons and what you can do to change your meeting status.

- *WHY YOU'RE NOT GETTING INVITED:* You're considered too young, too new, or too inexperienced. In other words, the powers that be may not feel that you bring a lot to the table at this point in your career, so they aren't going to shell out the bucks to send you to the annual client convention or risk sending you to meet with a bigwig before you've got more time under your belt.

SOLUTION: It's not your fault you're young, but you can begin to change people's perception of what you can contribute. Changing someone else's opinion—right or wrong—won't necessarily happen overnight, but when you are a competent professional—delivering quality work, dressing and acting professionally, showing up early to the job, or simply going beyond your job description—you'll show others that you do contribute at a high level, despite your age or lack of experience.

- *WHY YOU'RE NOT GETTING INVITED:* You haven't impressed them so far. Whether it's your dress, communication style, or simply the fact that you spend too much time text-messaging on your cell phone, you haven't given others a strong feeling of confidence in your abilities. And without that confidence, the boss isn't going to send you into a meeting with his peers, a client, or anyone else of import, and he probably isn't going to invest in sending you to the annual convention, either.

  SOLUTION: Accept responsibility—after all, if it's your behavior that is costing you opportunities, first admit what is really going on, then fix what isn't working. Tough though it may be, ask your boss for a few minutes to talk about what the issues are and how to improve: "Sarah, I noticed that I haven't been asked to attend many meetings with our client. Is there something that I can do or change so that I am able to attend more meetings in the future?"

- *WHY YOU'RE NOT GETTING INVITED:* They don't think you're ready yet. A slight variation on what we've shared earlier, this is a reason that comes up frequently when newer professionals ask why they've been left off the invite list. While you may be well respected and admired in the office, you may have yet to prove yourself in a certain area, and without the track record, you may not get a shot. Plus, your boss may be looking out for you—if you're not strong or are inexperienced in something, he doesn't want to risk embarrassing you in front of your coworkers, either.

SOLUTION: Stay one step ahead of them. For example, if you're the only member of the team who hasn't been asked to present at a meeting yet, join a public-speaking organization like Toastmasters and get some practice standing up in front of a group first. Then let your boss know that you've been working on your presentation skills and that you would like to be considered to give a brief presentation the next time the opportunity comes up.

"Dear Liz"

Meeting Situations Got You Stumped? Look No Further—Help Is Here!

Even when you've gotten a seat at the meeting table, things don't always go as planned. If you've found yourself in a tricky situation or two, don't despair—ask Liz for advice! Below, we've compiled some commonly asked questions and their responses, so you'll be able to handle whatever comes your way.

Dear Liz:

    Help! At a recent meeting, my boss kept asking me questions in front of everybody—and I had absolutely no idea what the answers were, even though I probably should have. What to do?

    Sincerely,

    Clueless Wonder

Dear Clueless Wonder:

Whenever you're asked a question and you really don't know the answer—even if you really should—don't try to BS your way out of it. Tempting though it may be to make something up on the spot that seems plausible, resist this urge. After all, you don't know what people will actually do with the answers you provide—and wouldn't it be a shame if your semi-accurate report of sales figures was actually printed in the company newsletter?

Instead, simply take a deep breath and say: "Jim, let me research that and get back to you and the group within the hour." On the other hand, you may not need to admit outright that you really have no clue what a particular answer is. For example, can you use what you *do* know to provide at least a partially correct response, and follow up on the rest? "Based on last year's performance, we were up about 4 percent at this time, but I'd really need to double-check where we are at currently before I can answer your question. I'll get that information to you after the meeting." You get the idea—simply let folks know that (1) you will get the answer, (2) you will share it with them, and (3) you will do all of this ASAP.

One other point, clueless friend: Getting stumped every once in a while is fine, but if you're always drawing a blank when questions come up, Liz thinks you might need to dust off the annual report or whatever else you need to brush up on your work IQ so you're as sharp as the rest of them.

Last but not least: Does your boss frequently ask you questions that are tough to answer in front of others? In other words, is she trying to make you look bad on purpose? Far be it from me to assume the worst, but Liz is wondering if your boss is trying to pull a fast one. Keep your eye on her—after all, her job is to support you, not make you look like a clueless wonder.

Dear Liz:

The meetings I attend are like boxing matches. People are competitive and nobody ever shuts up and lets anyone else get a word in edgewise. I hate office politics and am not the competitive type, so I wind up keeping quiet during the meetings—which makes me look like some kind of meeting loser. How do I still make a name for myself and get a word or two in without stooping to their level?

Sincerely,

Better Than the Idiots I Work With

Dear Better Than:

You're in a tricky situation, but you're not the only one. Unfortunately, meetings tend to bring out the worst in some of us. Maybe it's because we're all sitting around a table in close quarters, but meetings are places where we have a tendency to compare ourselves to others or where we measure our performance and our responses against those of our coworkers. If we play the comparison game and think we're coming up short, it's not pretty. So what to do?

As you recognized, you need to pipe up, but that doesn't mean you need to play dirty. If possible, see if you can get a formal spot on the agenda—that way, you're guaranteed a little time to speak, at the very least. But if not, you'll have to muscle your way in—strategically. For example, bring a handout or something on paper that is relevant to the meeting topic or agenda. When the moment seems right, get your paper ready and pounce: "Jim, let me step in for a minute, because you raise a great point. In fact, I noticed a similar issue in our recent newsletter, and I have copies here for you. If you'll turn to page two . . ."

You can also use this strategy throughout the meeting. If it's hard to get a word in edgewise, piggyback on the last comment you heard and transition into your idea—but don't worry if this doesn't always work. After all, when it comes to what you say at a meeting, quality, not quantity, is what really counts. Most of us wind up tuning out the coworkers who just love the sounds of their own voices, anyway, so don't feel like you have to keep score and say as much as the person sitting next to you.

One final thought: Keep in mind that the culture inside a meeting room usually reflects the culture of the workplace itself. If your office culture is a cutthroat one, it's no surprise that your meetings tend to be tough environments. Don't be afraid to use some of these same tactics outside of meetings to make sure you're gaining visibility in the workplace, too.

Dear Liz:

I try to stay awake . . . I try to pay attention . . . but you have no idea how boring the meetings are that I have to attend. How do I seem interested and engaged at these things—when I'm the farthest thing from it?

Sincerely,

Bored Beyond Recognition

Dear Bored:

You say you're bored at meetings?! No! The horror of it!!!

OK, forgive the sarcasm, but I think we both know

the answer to this one: Deal with it! This isn't to seem insensitive to your plight, but let's face it: If God wanted meetings to be exciting, he'd call them office parties. (Come to think of it, those can be boring, too. . . .)

Sure, Liz hates a boring meeting as much as the next employee, but consider the fact that meetings are designed to do many things—convey information, exchange ideas, solve problems—and getting employees excited and interested doesn't usually rank too high on the list, though it probably should. That said, there are things you can do to make meetings less painful. For starters, take notes. It may not sound thrilling, but it's better than doodling, which people do notice, and which also really broadcasts to the world how bored you are. Besides, when you go back to your desk after the meeting, you might find that the ideas you have on paper actually aren't so uninteresting—it was just the presenter of those ideas who bored you to tears.

While you're putting down your doodle pen, you'll also want to avoid playing with your BlackBerry or checking email on a laptop, text-messaging, or otherwise messing around with gadgets during a meeting. Not only is this rude, but it further removes you from the task at hand, so you're even more disengaged than you might be otherwise.

If you want to make meetings work for you, no matter how boring, have a plan in your mind about what you'd like to accomplish at each meeting. For instance, set a mini-goal for yourself to offer at least two new ideas or three solutions to existing problems at each meeting. If nothing else happens of interest, you'll have achieved something and come up with a few new ideas.

Finally, be part of the solution. If you're honestly bored, approach the meeting host ahead of time. Depending on the meeting, the attendees, and what you can bring to the table, why not offer to run a portion of the program? Tell the host you'd like to get more involved, and offer to volunteer your services to act as meeting facilitator or note taker, or play some other role where you'll have a "job" to keep you occupied. At the very least, offer to bring a few snacks for the group to munch on. You'd be amazed how a few pretzels can liven up even the dullest of affairs at work.

Step #5:
Master the Impromptu Workplace Meeting

Earlier in this chapter, we made a bold proclamation: Meetings happen everywhere . . . but most of us don't realize it. The truth is that meetings at work can go way beyond a gathering in a conference room with PowerPoint—but you've got to know where to look. Equally important, you've got to know how to act, so that when a meeting moment presents itself, you're ready to shine.

Prepare for Impromptu Meetings? Why Bother?

It's one thing to put the time and effort into a meeting you know you've got on the calendar—but for an impromptu meeting? Won't that mean we'd spend all of our time preparing for something that won't necessarily happen—and what about the other work we actually have to do during the workday?

Nobody is suggesting you abandon your work responsibilities so that you can prepare for the incredible meeting that is going to take place between you and the CEO . . . any day now. Instead, consider that "preparing" for an impromptu meeting isn't really something you have to do, because you already are prepared . . . *if* you're already showing up to work acting professionally and dressing sharp, with your eye on the ball.

Impromptu meeting preparation simply means being ready for anything, because you never really know when a good opportunity might present itself. In other words, you have to develop the mind-set that every day is "game day." At any moment, you might have a rare one-on-one opportunity to chat with the CEO or strike up a conversation with a senior-level coworker, and you want to be ready to talk about something besides the weather or the great lasagna they are serving for lunch downstairs in the cafeteria when those moments happen.

Plus, impromptu meetings are worth their weight in gold, because of their spur-of-the-moment qualities. The reality is that you aren't getting on the CEO's meeting agenda anytime soon, but you might be able to exchange a few ideas with him in the hallway at work. You may not have many opportunities to see your work world beyond your cubicle, besides interacting with your boss and a few coworkers, and you might not be included in a lot of meetings or other company events early in your career. The impromptu meeting may be the only game left in town for you, and you've got to strike when you can—that's why professionalism and preparation go hand in hand. When you're ready for game day, you're ready to use the impromptu meeting to take advantage of unique opportunities that you wouldn't otherwise have access to.

Impromptu Meetings: Where Are They?

Meetings can happen at any time once you develop the mind-set and awareness that a meeting is really about exchanging ideas, information, insights, or anything else that allows you and your coworkers to solve problems or generate new solutions to perform your jobs at a higher level. In other words, a meeting isn't chatting about last night's episode of *American Idol* at the water cooler—think of it as a strategic, purposeful conversation that can take place almost anywhere, including:

- A restaurant
- The company cafeteria
- The lobby of your office building
- An elevator
- The hallway at work
- The kitchen on your floor at work
- The train as you commute to and from work
- A bar or anyplace you go for drinks after work
- The company softball game

You get the picture. In one case, Andrew, a director of client services at a Boston-based financial services company, briefly introduced himself to the New York–based CEO and other senior-level management of his organization after the company held an off-site "town hall" meeting one morning. He realized that the executive team needed to leave the meeting venue and head over to the Boston office, but they were unfamiliar with the route, so he offered to show them where they needed to go. They appreciated his gesture, and, in the meantime, Andrew had several minutes to exchange ideas with some of the top leaders in his organization. (By the way, he wouldn't have had this opportunity at all if he hadn't taken the initiative to introduce himself after the town hall meeting in the first place, so keep those introductions coming.)

Once you step out of your cubicle, meetings can happen anytime you take the initiative to make them happen. This isn't to suggest that you approach the vice president of marketing in the restroom and ask about the upcoming advertising campaign across the urinals, or that you walk around the office all day trying to strike up purposeful conversations with people. After all, we all have a job to do, and not everyone wants a part in your impromptu meeting when trying to meet a deadline.

When NOT to Make a Meeting Happen

Be careful when discussing matters of work in public settings. This isn't to suggest that you can't strike up a purposeful conversation with a coworker on the train that you both commute on to and from work, but make sure you respect the rules your company has set around confidentiality. Whether you're in the company elevator, at a restaurant, or anyplace else beyond your employer's walls, be aware of the fact that you really don't know who else might be listening in on your seemingly innocent chat. Just ask Brooke, a 28-year-old account executive at a large advertising agency: "I was at lunch with two coworkers and we were talking about a difficult client and how to handle an upcoming presentation for them. As we got up to leave the restaurant, we noticed that three people from our client's office were dining only two tables away. Fortunately, the restaurant was pretty loud, and we don't think they heard us, but it was a very close call."

The moral of the story? When it comes to where to hold a

meeting, use your best judgment. In other words, talking about
last quarter's figures in the elevator with your VP of finance—
and 10 other people from other companies who happen to work
in your office building—is a no-no.

Impromptu Meeting Tips: How to Act

When it comes to the informal or impromptu meetings we've
just described, it's important to handle yourself as professionally as you would inside a meeting room. How to make
the most of these opportunities? Consider these tips.

- *DRESS SHARP.* We'll say it again and again: Appearance
  counts. How "strategic" is that meeting of yours going to
  be when your coworkers are distracted by the thong
  peeking out of your pants? When the meeting is over,
  what will they really remember about your conversation?

- *HAVE SOME IDEAS READY IN YOUR BACK POCKET.* You
  don't want to sound forced or unnatural, but there is
  nothing wrong with having a few facts, figures, or other
  notes jotted down on an index card or in your PalmPilot
  so that you'll still have a few things to say if you get
  tongue-tied or simply forget your thoughts.

- *FOLLOW UP.* Your impromptu meeting could be the beginning of something beautiful, so don't let the magic end
  once your meeting is over. Send a follow-up email or voice
  mail that reminds your meeting mate of what you discussed
  and of action items. Or, when your meeting is finished, ask
  for a chance to schedule a more formal second meeting.
  Above all, thank the person for their time, always.

- *LOOP OTHERS IN—ESPECIALLY YOUR BOSS.* If you were fortunate enough to have a terrific impromptu meeting with a company bigwig, let your boss in on the action. At the very least, don't forget to drop your boss's name during your conversation once or twice, so the big shots know whom you report to. After your meeting, let your boss know what transpired, too. And finally, when you send that thank-you or follow-up email, be sure to copy your boss on the communication, and include him or her in a follow-up meeting.

- *HAVE COURAGE.* You might come into contact with plenty of interesting executives, hardworking coworkers, or other colleagues with whom you can exchange ideas—as long as you are willing to approach them first. Don't expect others to come to you or take the initiative when it comes to an impromptu meeting. It's up to you to get the ball rolling, so take a deep breath, and go for it.

Whether you're attending dozens of meetings each week or once in a blue moon, it's up to you to make the most of these opportunities to shine. Meetings equal visibility, so it's important to understand how meetings can help you, so that you are visible and remembered in the way you want to be. Think of meetings as the ultimate secret weapon at work—they can make a big difference in your career, and most people aren't even clued in to how helpful they can actually be. When you approach meetings with the right mind-set, when you prepare so that you're not caught off guard, and when you have a game plan so that you're ready to really make the most of your time with others, you give yourself and your career a big advantage in the workplace.

SECTION II

Relationships at Work

UNSPOKEN RULE #4

Don't Assume You Said (or Wrote) What You Meant

Sound as Good as You Look by Mastering the Art of Business Communication

Introduction:
Why Communication Matters So Much on the Job

Communication—whether verbal or written—causes many a mess and misunderstanding on the job. But it doesn't have to be this way. By being a good listener, a smart emailer, a witty conversationalist, a persuasive presenter, and a halfway decent writer, you can rise above the communication madness and stand out in the crowd. Sounds like a tall order? Trust me, you can handle this. Don't believe me? Just look at what's inside your own workplace. For instance, when was the last time you read your organization's mission statement? Did it inspire you . . . or confuse you? If you're worried you can't handle the communication challenge, reread a few of your company's catchphrases and tell yourself that you can't do much worse.

Why is it so important to communicate effectively, particularly when it comes to email? Studies show that email—by far—rules the workplace when it comes to how employees prefer to communicate. But you don't need a study to tell you this; after all, about 98 percent of Americans at work use email (sorry, that's another study for you), and 48 percent of employees report that the number of emails they send and receive in the workplace increases annually, according to a 2002 Pew Charitable Trust Internet Report. Let's not even talk about the study that revealed that over 60 billion emails

worldwide were estimated to be sent daily in 2006, according to industry analysts (www.vnunet.com/vnunet/news/
2120233/mail-31-billion-day). Yikes! Where is that delete
button!?

Sure, it doesn't take a rocket scientist to point out why we
love email, but life on the job gets a bit trickier when you
consider that the very things we love about this convenient,
time-saving tool are often the same things that have caused
problems on the job. Hopefully, you're sending messages
that reflect your best, but if you're like most of us, you may
have created one or two along the way that you'd like to
delete forever, if only you could. Read on to learn how to
make your emails even better, starting now.

Step #1:
Create Compelling Emails that Actually Get Read

Email is so useful, so helpful, and so necessary in today's
workplace that it almost seems unholy to criticize it or call it
something as dramatic as a double-edged sword. But that's
exactly what it is—and the very same tool that makes you a
hero at work can also be the one that can stab you in the
back when you least expect it. Here's why.

It's Easy—and That's the Problem

It's too easy. It's too easy to dash off an email to a coworker
when you're feeling ticked off, only to regret it enormously
seconds later. It's too easy to write an email with poor grammar, misspellings, or incorrect information, making you look
like a less intelligent, less educated version of yourself. It's

too easy to send an email to anyone, anytime, about nearly anything, which is why we all get so much pointless, dumb, useless email that clogs our in-boxes and wastes hours upon hours of productivity.

Because it's so darn easy to send an email, we do, sometimes without thinking. And the consequences of this can run from mild to extremely serious. For example:

- Consider the email sent by the first-year law associate at one of New York's most prestigious law firms: He wrote to friends bragging about wasting time on the company dime, expensing pricey sushi lunches, and so on. Perhaps it was the especially obnoxious, arrogant tone of his emails that caused them to get passed around . . . and around . . . and around, to the point where they were reprinted in the *Wall Street Journal.* Think his boss found out about that one?

- We've all heard horror stories about the employee who thinks she is sending her friends a grouchy email complaining about her boss, only to discover in horror that she accidentally sent the very email *to* her boss. There are dozens of variations on this mishap—like the employee who sends a confidential email to the entire company, by accident, and so on. These aren't just urban legends—I worked with someone who was fired because he sent an off-color joke to the entire organization, when he only intended it for a select audience.

- One of my favorite email stories comes from Ashley, a senior-level manager at a financial services company, who still remembers the email she received (along with everyone on her team) from the new employee who had just graduated from college. Despite the fact that he had only been on the job for a few weeks, the newbie felt compelled to offer his work suggestions to the group in a 1500-word email, which outlined everything from his thoughts on dress code to ideas for improving employee morale. For months, his email was circulated internally and became the butt of jokes around the office, with people wondering how this new guy could have been so clueless.

The moral of the story? It's easy to let email hurt your career—easier than any of us might think when we're dashing off a quick message to a few friends. It's also easy to think that we'd never perform this kind of dumb behavior or that we would never be so misguided as to send an unprofessional email like the ones outlined above. Still, before you congratulate yourself too heartily, notice that nobody necessarily plans these brilliant moves on purpose—but when all it takes is a point and a click, no wonder so many of us have accidentally sent the wrong things to the wrong people at one point or another. Most of us don't think that our emails sound idiotic—in fact, they often look quite brilliant on the screen. It isn't until you get raised eyebrows and surprised looks around the office that you begin to see that your inspired email may have not been received exactly in the way it was intended.

The Other Problem with Email: It's "Empowering"

Similar to the line of thinking that says "Well, I called her last time; now it's her turn to call me back," sending out email can put us on moral high ground, at least temporarily. In a small way, dashing off an email lets us feel that we're in the right and that it isn't our problem if something doesn't get accomplished. After all, you've done your part, and it isn't your fault if people haven't gotten back to you yet. As a result, the "proactive" move we've made becomes a passive one, where we delay taking action and wait for the powers that be to get back to us before we take the next steps.

Naturally, we're not suggesting that you don't get feedback or the appropriate approvals, or that you simply charge ahead on your next project, full speed, without getting the buy-in you need via email or some other channel. We're also not proposing a temporary ban on emails—among their millions of other useful qualities, emails provide a written record, a confirmation on paper (or the computer screen) of what was said, of what needs to be done, of what was agreed upon, and so on: a critically important quality that other modes of communication, like voice mails and conversations, can't offer. Instead, simply consider the degree to which email allows us to take action on the job—or gives us an excuse to sit behind our desks.

In other words, email is no substitute for picking up the phone, getting out of your chair, and walking down the hall to speak with someone, and, yes, actually going to the trouble of scheduling a face-to-face meeting with 10 other people, as logistically annoying as that may be. Sometimes it's those kinds of things that are needed when it comes to getting the job done. It's so easy to rely on email that we tend to overly rely on it, and get lazy when it comes to developing and using the other skills that really do get things accomplished—like networking, relationship-building, and navigating through office politics and bureaucracy. Dealing with people is hard work, and sometimes it feels so much easier to just send an email instead—but this does anything but empower us and our careers.

Step #2:
Avoid On-Screen Blunders, Pitfalls, and Career-Ending Email Disasters

Sending Emails the Workplace Way: Dos and Don'ts for Communication

Consider a few other pointers for delivering a winning email below.

DO *DECIDE WHETHER YOU NEED TO SEND OUT AN EMAIL AT ALL.* A general rule of thumb? If it takes you longer than 10 minutes to type it out, it's probably too long for an email, and other modes of communication (conference call, memo, meetings) may be required. Plus, most people just don't have time for your long emails, anyway.

DO *REMEMBER THAT THERE ARE JUST SOME THINGS THAT NEVER BELONG IN AN EMAIL.* Salary-related issues should always be discussed in person, and only with your manager or HR Department. And keep other sensitive issues out. As one advertising employee put it: "Write every email as if it was splashed across the front page of the *New York Times*." Things get forwarded around, emails that you thought were confidential become fodder for public discussion; so when it doubt, leave it out.

DO *BE CONSCIOUS OF THE TONE YOUR EMAILS CONVEY.* "Many younger employees around the office send

emails with no "Dear So-and-So," or even "Hello." Even
if they don't intend it, it comes across as short and im-
polite at times," says Dale Kalman, vice president of
stock plan services at Charles Schwab. "I also had a situation where a newer employee sent a client an email
that came across as arrogant. The client forwarded the
email to me, commenting that he was surprised that a
service-oriented company like ours could have sent an
email like this. Needless to say, that email hurt our relationship with that client and cost us money."

DO *MAKE LIFE EASY FOR YOUR EMAIL READERS.* Use
numbers, lists, bullet points—they help break up the
content and ensure that your ideas don't get buried in
long paragraphs, which we tend to skim over and ab-
sorb minimally.

DO *ASK YOUR MANAGER OR A TRUSTED COWORKER
ABOUT WHO ELSE SHOULD BE RECEIVING YOUR EMAILS
IF YOU'RE UNSURE.* No, it isn't a crime to send your
email to one or two people who may not necessarily
need to read it—unless your email contains confidential or other proprietary information that isn't for
everyone's eyes. However, people tend to get a bit
cranky and ticked off when they continue to receive
emails from people they don't know or about stuff
they don't have any involvement with.

DO *PROOFREAD YOUR EMAILS FIRST.* We all know
we're supposed to do this one, but how many emails
do you receive in a day with typos, misspellings, funky
punctuation, all lowercase letters, poor grammar, or
other gaffes? Not only do mistakes make emails

tougher to read and harder to follow (because we're secretly wondering why you don't know the difference between "you're" and "your" instead of reading your message), but they make you look bad, too. It only takes a minute to use spell-check and look your messages over before sending them out, and it can make a world of difference for you and your readers.

DO *WAIT UNTIL THE LAST MINUTE TO PUT YOUR RECIPIENTS IN THE "TO" LINE IN YOUR EMAILS.* Technology is tricky, and it's easy for anyone to accidentally hit the send button before your email is really fit for human consumption and in any kind of condition to be read by others, let alone your boss. Give yourself some built-in protection by writing the email first and addressing it last so that you don't send your message before it's really ready.

DO *THINK TWICE BEFORE SENDING ATTACHMENTS.* Unless you've told your email recipients in advance (particularly those to whom your email is being sent externally), many people opt not to open anything unfamiliar, rather than risk letting a virus or other bug onto their computer. Plus, we're overloaded with information, and clicking on an attachment is just one more thing we have to do. Post your attachment on your company's intranet instead, for instance, and send a hyperlink to the document in the body of the email, and chances are far more likely you'll have people reading what you intended.

DO *KNOW THE RULES OF YOUR WORKPLACE WHEN IT COMES TO EMAIL.* Many offices have strict policies about sending personal (non-work-related) email from work and also have guidelines about email content itself. Remember, it's perfectly legal for your company to monitor (e.g., read) your work email and IM content and tell you exactly how and how not to use your computer, so make sure you're on the right side of the law when it comes to what you communicate.

DO *BE BRIEF.* Remember, nothing makes your coworkers reach for the delete button faster than a long, drawn-out email. The shorter, the better. If you must send out a bunch of information, divide it into separate emails, so that you don't overwhelm everyone at once.

DON'T *USE WEIRD FONTS,* elaborate graphics, inspirational quotes, funky colors, or anything else that makes your communication tough to read, hard to open, or just plain annoying. While you're at it, skip the ALL CAPS (makes people feel like you're shouting at them) or all lowercase (gives people the sense that you are mumbling), and use bold and underline functions with discretion—too much is overkill, and makes readers feel like you're talking at them, not with them.

DON'T *EMAIL WHEN YOU'RE FEELING ANYTHING LESS THAN AN 8 ON A SANITY SCALE OF 1 TO 10 AT WORK.* If you're angry, frustrated, shortchanged, underappreciated, devalued, or just want to have a meltdown and scream, stop. Walk away from the computer, take a deep breath, and count to 10 (or, better yet, 10,000) before you even think of emailing anything to anyone. An email written in an emotional moment can cause plenty of heartache for you later on—it's just not worth it.

DON'T *SEND YOUR EMAIL TO EVERYONE WITH A HEARTBEAT,* and use "reply all" with care. For political reasons, or simply to cover our own behinds, we tend to send out our emails to far more people than is really necessary. Add up the recipients, carbon copies, and blind carbon copies, and you've sent that email to half the state of Utah. Our philosophy? Less is more, at least when it comes to your email list. If you panic at the thought of leaving somebody off an email, include the following at the bottom of your message: "Please forward this email to anyone that I've missed. Thanks."

DON'T *HESITATE TO BRING OTHER PEOPLE INTO YOUR PROOFREADING PARTY,* either, when it comes to important emails. Before you hit the send button, ask your manager, when appropriate, or a trusted colleague to take a look at your brilliant email before everyone else gets to see it. Not only will they catch mistakes that you may have missed, but they'll also be able to judge the message for content or ideas, and give it a general thumbs-up—or not.

DON'T *FORWARD THE HARMLESS JOKES,* the political cartoons, or anything else that isn't work-related. Delete this stuff that gets emailed to you, even if it seems perfectly OK. Many an employee has been undone by forwarding an innocent story or joke, only to be told by HR that their email constitutes sexual harassment or is contributing to a hostile work environment. What seems funny to you may not to someone you work with—and it's not worth the time, effort, or risk to your career to deal with that headache.

And last, but not least . . .

DON'T *FORGET THAT YOUR EMAILS AREN'T GOING ANYWHERE.* Maybe we've all seen one too many episodes of *CSI,* but you and I know that you can delete all you want and there will still be a copy of your email saved somewhere in the depths of your computer till kingdom come. Before you hit the send button, do you really want a permanent record of whatever it is you're about to communicate? If so, hit send. But if the feeling in your gut tells you otherwise, best get the delete button ready and forget the email before it ever sees the light of day. As Kevin Giglinto, vice president of sales and marketing of the Chicago Symphony Orchestra, adds, "Never send emails on the company server unless they are constructive or professional. I've seen people get fired for the mistaken circulation of emails or from other people forwarding something they didn't realize was private. It isn't worth risking your career, and the wrong kind of email can do just that."

Word Up!
A Note about Microsoft Word Attachments

Think twice before sending Microsoft Word documents as attachments. Computer-savvy readers already know that Microsoft Word documents can be saved with the "track changes" option enabled. If the document is saved in this way, every edit and change that you and others have made can be viewed. While this can be a helpful option, particularly when working on a document with a group of coworkers, it can also open up a can of worms under different circumstances.

For instance, imagine that you're sending a contract to a client, and you've changed the price tag on the document from $5,000 to $7,500. With a few clicks, the client can easily see the previously lower price tag in the attachment. Some organizations have other concerns with Word attachments—namely, that they are one of the most common avenues through which viruses are sent. Another concern is that in order to view Word documents, the recipient must also have Microsoft Word, which is not always the case. To be on the safe side, save Word documents as .rtf or .pdf files before attaching them to your message, and leave the Word documents for other purposes.

Step #3:
Understand Why They Aren't Reading Your Emails—and What to Do about It

Given the thousands of emails that are flying around your office on a daily basis, it's easy to have your emails ignored, deleted, or put on the back burner, whether you realize it is happening to you or not. At the very least, it's frustrating to know that the time and effort you're putting into emails and other written communications is going to waste. On a more serious note, ignored emails can cost you money and hurt your career.

Why would somebody ignore your emails and other writ-

ten communication—and what does it take to get them noticed? Read on for our strategies and solutions.

- *YOUR EMAILS ARE GETTING IGNORED BECAUSE . . .* you
  haven't given readers a compelling enough reason to
  open your message.

  SOLUTION: Create a subject line that grabs readers and
  compels them to take action. Even if you're sending an
  email to the boss, make sure that your subject line helps
  her clearly see (1) the content of your email and (2) what
  action you need her to take. Even something as simple as
  "Need Your Approval on Paragraph 3 of Attached
  Brochure" in the subject line can do the trick. When subject lines are boring, nondescriptive, or blank, we just
  don't have enough information or interest to necessarily
  want to go further and actually read the message. One
  note: Be sure to remove all caps, exclamation points, or
  words like "free" in your subject line—otherwise, your
  emails may get filtered out as spam.

- *YOUR EMAILS AREN'T GETTING READ BECAUSE . . .* we
  don't know who you are. Today, it's fairly common practice to delete or ignore personal emails we receive from
  strangers, but don't assume the same thing isn't going on
  in the workplace, where busy people may not have the
  time or inclination to open emails from people they don't
  know.

  SOLUTION: In the subject line, make it very clear who you
  are and what you want: "New Assistant for John Smith
  Seeking Your Approval on Upcoming Mailing" can do the
  trick, and a slightly longer subject line may be a helpful
  attention-getter (provided it's written in a compelling,

professional manner). If that doesn't work, follow up your emails with a phone call or voice mail if you don't hear back within a reasonable amount of time: "Hi, Alice. We haven't met, but I'm John Smith's new assistant, and I wanted to follow up with you regarding the email I sent on . . ." In your voice mail, be sure to give your precise email address and the exact date on which you sent your email—this makes it much easier for people to go back into their files and find your message.

And if they are still getting ignored? Send a memo, letter, or handwritten note instead. In today's email-dominated workplace, you'd be surprised how much written communication stands out and is appreciated.

- *YOUR EMAILS AND OTHER WRITTEN COMMUNICATIONS ARE GETTING THE SHAFT BECAUSE* . . . they are unprofessional. If you're producing work that is sloppy, inappropriate, or contains plenty of typos or grammatical mistakes, you're not doing yourself any favors, and you're reinforcing a less-than-ideal impression in the minds of others every single time you send out a message. If people start to associate you with undesirable stuff, they may also make the same connection when it comes to your written work and assume—fairly or not—that you don't have anything of value to offer.

SOLUTION: Like every other aspect of building your reputation, it takes time to build up something you're proud of—and even more time to undo any damage you may have done. Start over by asking people at work, including your boss, for an honest assessment of your emails, memos, or anything else you're writing on a regular basis. Print out copies of a few you've sent over the past months and get some feedback. (This is also a good strategy even if you've never run into issues with email—you never know what coworkers might notice that you've been missing all these months.) Then take their advice, and ask them to keep proofreading the next time you want to hit the send button for something important.

While you're at it, become a student of how your boss and his peers communicate. Read and reread their emails, pay attention to how they write, and adapt their style and techniques in your own way to polish up your messages, too.

Keep in mind that even the best of us get emails and other documents ignored—so try not to take it personally. Many employees receive so many emails in a day that there is simply no way to keep up and read them all. Others work in organizations with such tight email security that a message from the Pope couldn't get through, so don't be surprised if some kind of spam filter got rid of your email before anyone even had a chance to look at it.

As you can see, sending out an email that contributes to your success isn't quite as simple as hitting the send button. With only a little extra thought and time devoted to the emails you send, you give yourself—and your career— an important edge.

To End or Not to End: That Is the Question

Let's face it: Some emails just don't need to be sent, like the "thank you!" email in response to the "thank you!" that was in response to the "OK!" that was in response to the "Talk to you next week," and on it goes. If you've ever been caught in an email discussion like this one, you know ending email conversations can be tough. Unlike a phone call or a face-to-face conversation, we can't necessarily use tone or body language or even eye contact as clues that a conversation is winding down and coming to a close. As a result, things can get awkward and weird when trying to say goodbye, because the last thing we want to do is seem rude when we don't reply to someone's "OK," and so we get caught in the annoying web of sending email after email. Our advice? Don't respond once it's clear the crux of the conversation is over. After all, somebody's got to end the pointless banter—why not you? Look, nobody likes a grouch, but enough already. Life is too short to be sending out "OK!" and "Sounds good!" all day long.

Step #4:
IM Talking to You! Sound Smart and Play It Safe When Using IM at Work

You either love it or hate it: I'm talking about instant messaging, or IM, the not-so-latest communication tool that allows you to converse online in real time. IM has a strong fan base, which is only growing within the workplace; meanwhile, just as many employees find the tool irritating and time-wasting. Regardless of where you fall on the IM spectrum, check out the tips below to be ready when the urge to IM hits.

- IM is for quick, casual questions, brief updates, or short, time-sensitive bits of communication. Keep your messages short and sweet—anything more than a sentence or two belongs in an email.

- IM is real time, so write with caution. Like email, you've got a record of everything you're writing; be sure you're putting down something on screen that you wouldn't mind anyone else in your organization reading.

- Use a professional screen name—so "CoolieJulie" and "Monkeyboy" are out. While you're at it, don't overdo the IM-speak and abbreviations. IM jargon and slang aren't standardized, and you may lose people who aren't necessarily operating on the same page as you. To be safe and understood, stick to using real words.

- Get right into your subject matter. "How are you?" may add only a minute or two to your IM conversation—but multiply that by the number of times you IM during the day, and that can mean plenty of wasted time. A simple: "Have time for a quick question?" to get the ball rolling is pleasant enough, and cuts to the chase.

- When you're IMing, be aware that you may be catching someone in the middle of something, like a meeting, or your conversation may be cut short if the phone rings, so don't be surprised if you get a long pause (or very long pause) before you receive a reply from the other end of the screen. Also, remember that you may be IMing someone who is not alone in their cubicle or office—so all the more reason to take care with your messages.

- Be a grown-up. One finance manager reports that his newer employees thought it was cute to sneak over to a coworker's desk while he had stepped away and type silly or inappropriate IM messages to others. Others love IM because it allows them to communicate and gossip about coworkers without coworkers hearing the conversation going on. It should go without saying, but don't mess with other people's IM (or computers, for that matter), and take the high road when it comes to IM. Do you really want to have to explain to HR or your boss what you were up to if you were actually caught doing this second-grade stuff? While you're at it, shut down your own IM when you're away from your desk to keep the pranksters out.

- Turn it off. Well-meaning friends may pop in, pop up, and say hi at any given moment of the day with IM, but there are times when you need to focus, want to concentrate, or simply are in a bad mood and don't want to be interrupted, so don't hesitate to turn off your IM program if needed or use some other common IM features, like "busy" or "away," to indicate you're not free to chat. And respect the space of others, too: Just because someone is online doesn't mean they have time to IM with you—so be smart and don't overdo it, either.

- Don't let IM become a substitute for verbal, face-to-face communication. Dale Kalman of Charles Schwab has opted not to make IM available to the 120 employees in his department. "With IM, you lose any opportunity to learn how to really develop and manage business relationships in any kind of sophisticated, complex way. My employees need to learn how to really talk to clients, and IM just wasn't giving them that training."

Communication—
Going beyond the Computer Screen

If you're smart enough to know how to send an email, you're also savvy enough to know that good communication goes way beyond your computer screen.

When it comes to exchanging ideas, sharing information, speaking, listening, and really being understood and understanding others in the workplace, email and IM are only the tip of the iceberg. After all, there are newsletters, memos, letters, meetings, phone calls, conferences, training programs, and retreats, not to mention actual, real conversations between people that happen countless times throughout any given office on any given day. While any of these tools can serve as an important communication vehicle, none is perhaps quite so challenging, so confounding, and so darn difficult as the good, old-fashioned face-to-face conversation, dialogue, or other verbal discussion. How do we communicate with each other in a way that really does get the job done—and keeps us happy—at the same time?

Step #5:
Communicate Like a Pro—Dealing with Difficult (or Deranged) Communicators

As you already know and undoubtedly have experienced, not everyone is born knowing how to communicate effectively . . . or at all. After all, our goal is to be the kind of person who knows how to deliver ideas and messages in a way that resonates with other people, who can handle himself in a one-on-one conversation with a peer . . . or a manager . . . or a CFO. I'm pointing to the person who commands respect when she opens her mouth to share an idea—instead of making other people wince, whine, or simply tune out. Now *that's* communication.

Effective communication isn't about dominating the meeting, the conversation, or the room—instead, it's really about your ability to get others to listen to you and, yes, to like

you. Sound easy? How often do you really listen to others—
and genuinely like them? This isn't to suggest that the workplace is filled with cranky nonlisteners or that life is about
winning the approval of others, but poor communication
skills are one of the fastest ways I know to turn off just about
anybody and dramatically shorten your list of friends—not to
mention hurt your career. Strong communication skills are
also priority numero uno when it comes to what employers
are looking for in new hires. According to the National
Association of Colleges and Employers *Job Outlook 2006* report, communication skills consistently rank as the most important quality or skill companies look for in potential
employees—and this has been the case for the past 10 years.
However, employers also say that this same skill is sorely
lacking in the candidates they eventually hire. In fact, according to one survey, nearly 70 percent of employers today
are "fed up" with how their employees talk, dress, and, yes,
communicate.

The moral of the story? Those of us who are able to master the art of communication have an advantage in our careers that the rest of us won't—but the key is being clued in
enough about ourselves to know when we're communicating like a pro and when we're not, so we're able to improve
where and when we need to. After all, you can sound sharp
on paper or in an email, but if you can't convey that same
sense of professionalism and polish when you're actually
speaking with someone else—whether it's in a job interview,
a meeting, or a simple one-on-one conversation with your
boss or some coworkers—you and your career will feel
some pain. Let's face it: Communication is about interaction,
and if people don't want to interact with you, they just won't
want to work with you, let alone spend time with you. And
that's a rough way to spend a day at work.

Handle Your Coworkers Like a Pro

It's one thing to want to be a better communicator—after all, we know that people with better speaking and presentation skills tend to be considered for leadership opportunities and promotions above their coworkers. In fact, surveys also reveal that the employee with the better communication skills will be promoted before a coworker who may otherwise possess stronger qualifications. Knowing how closely communication skills are linked to career success, you'd think that everyone would want to master them. But we know better. All it takes is spending a day or two on the job to realize that some people simply aren't clued in to how difficult or annoying their communication style is to the rest of us, and unless you happen to be the offender's manager, it isn't necessarily your job to show them the error of their ways.

However, if you happen to work with someone who has a communication style that is preventing you from getting your job done, making life on the job truly difficult, or just plain driving you nuts, you aren't completely stuck or powerless. In fact, you've got options for dealing with difficult communicators beyond ignoring them, hoping they'll get transferred to Brazil, or simply praying that they will get a clue on their own or that someone else will clue them in to how irritating they are. Sorry, friend, if none of the above has happened yet, you owe it to yourself, your career, and your sanity to deal with the tricky communicator with the best weapon you've got—your own terrific communication skills.

The good news is that there are plenty of effective communication strategies you can use when working with difficult communicators, but tread carefully. After all, it is a manager's job (or the job of Human Resources) to deal with employees who are genuinely offending and disrupting others, not yours. But realistically, you and I aren't going to run to the boss every time Chatty Patty comes strolling into our cubicle to shoot the breeze for 45 minutes when we're under a deadline—we've got to figure out a way to deal with it.

The key is to remember that you're not giving advice or trying to "correct" someone else—that kind of stuff doesn't go over well, particularly when you're new to the job or one of the younger employees in the workplace. After all, we don't want to be known as the communicator who thinks we're better than everyone else, do we? As Kevin Giglinto, vice president of sales and marketing of the Chicago Symphony Orchestra, points out, "Sometimes when you are in a job, you are performing, like an actor. You have a role to play and you need to play it to get the bigger role down the road. Even if people are horrible, never show your cards or wear your emotions on your sleeve."

Read on and consider how you can handle a few challenging communication styles in a manner that is friendly, diplomatic, and professional and doesn't cause you—or the offender—too much pain.

Communication Style #1: The Oversharer

Know any Oversharers? Sure you do, and you probably know way more about them than you'd like, too. Consider the Oversharer I met one day when running a training program at a company. A latecomer entered the room and in front of about 50 people, this employee apologized for being late, and then proceeded to tell us about how she suffered from ADD and depression and had a big fight with her daughter that morning, which is why she was tardy. Did I mention this was in front of *50 people*?

DEALING WITH AN OVERSHARER: It's one thing to hear the occasional tidbit of juicy gossip or get some interesting news from a friend at work; it's another to get a first-person account of someone's latest work or life drama when you'd rather know nothing. Nip this situation in the bud before your Oversharer starts revealing details about his latest colonoscopy. The minute a coworker crosses a line and starts sharing information with you that is best said to family or close friends, try, "Jean, I'm sure you have friends who are more qualified than me to talk about stuff like that." Try a version of this that sounds the most natural to you, but move on—and fast.

Communication Style #2: The Cliff Clavin
If you've ever seen reruns of *Cheers,* then you remember Cliff Clavin, the know-it-all postal worker who sat on a barstool and added his two cents to everything and everyone. Cliff had a knack for getting a word in edgewise, and always had to be right—even when he was wrong—and Cliffs roam the workplace everywhere, to one degree or another. You might run into Cliff in a meeting—that's the coworker who always has to add his point of view or elaborate on a point someone else has made. You may sit next to Cliff at the office, where you're treated to words of wisdom all day long on everything from computer software to choosing your next car.

HANDLING CLIFF: Like the Oversharer, the Cliff Clavins of the world need a partner in crime, so if you don't engage in a dialogue or give them too much attention, they'll find someone else who will and leave you alone. If Cliff offers you his opinion about why your next project won't work or why mustard is the new ketchup, try: *"Hmmm."* Yes, that's right—don't respond, literally. After all, Cliffs are so desperate to prove their genius to the rest of us that all it takes is a word or two from you to get them going. If that seems too extreme, use as few words as possible—no matter what he comments on. Phrases like *"Oh, really,"* *"Wow,"* or *"Good to know"* can all do the trick. Whatever you say, resist the urge to debate, get into a discussion, or offer up your two cents in kind—otherwise, you'll never get rid of him.

Communication Style #3: The Cubicle Invader
Run, hide, here comes a Cubicle Invader! They're everywhere, in every type of workplace imaginable—they might be in your cubicle right now. Just look for the person, other than you, who is in your cubicle almost as often as you are, and you'll know you've got an Invader on your hands. Why, you might ask, have you been the lucky one chosen by the Invader? Who knows—maybe your cubicle is a temporary escape, allowing the Invader to hide, albeit briefly, from his boss and the responsibilities of the day. Or maybe your cubicle has a better view, or better snacks, than that of your Invader—the point is, you've got someone who likes to hang out in your workspace, frequently, and usually without invitation.

This is the coworker who uses verbal and nonverbal communication to irritate—after all, when you're trying to get work done in a fairly small space, it makes life considerably more difficult to have an unofficial roommate hogging up square footage and going on and on about who knows what. Plus, Cubicle Invaders tend to be snoopy little devils—they love to peek at our computer screens or even rummage through our papers to see what we're up to—a particularly dicey situation when we've got confidential paperwork that we don't want others to see.

DEALING WITH THE CUBICLE INVADER: The best strategy for dealing with a Cubicle Invader is not letting them invade in the first place. If you've got an office, shutting your door may be all it takes to get the job done. Otherwise, put a strip of masking tape across your cubicle entranceway for a "do not disturb" look. Don't worry about looking antisocial here, as long as you don't do this too often; plenty of employees have used this technique to keep folks out from time to time. But if you turn around in your chair and find you've already been invaded, do what you can to get rid of this person: "Mark, listen, I have *got* to finish this. Let me give you a call when I'm done."

Remember, Cubicle Invaders don't understand concepts like personal space and boundaries like the rest of us do, so be straightforward. You don't want to be too harsh or hurt anyone's feelings in the process, but if you're too nice, they might never leave, so strike a balance and move on. And while you're at it, put the confidential papers away and invest in a file cabinet that locks, so you've got less to worry about when Snoopy drops in for a visit next time.

Communication Style #4: The Whiner
If you're being driven crazy by a Whiner, rest assured you're not the only one—these folks bug everyone, from the Whiner's boss to the company cafeteria worker who serves him eggs (that are probably too cold, too hot, or too something). Whiners at work are like Whiners anywhere—people who have never found something they couldn't complain about, and want the rest of us to know all about it.

DEALING WITH A WHINER: If you're in the misfortunate situation of working closely with a Whiner, pass the buck whenever possible. Like some of the other communication styles you may have to deal with, the Whiner is another great example of "less is more"—the less you say, the more success you'll probably have in getting away from this person. If she's complaining about a project at work, say: "Alice, this seems to be really important to you. Why don't you bring it up with your manager?" If she's whining about her salary, suggest: "Maybe you should discuss this with HR." Of course, the Whiner probably won't actually do anything, but at least you've made the point that you have no interest in hearing this stuff and that the Whiner should find someone else to complain to.

If you happen to be working with someone whose communication style is less than desirable, don't be afraid to handle the situation in a way that's appropriate, professional, and diplomatic. As you've noted with all the situations above, don't make life on the job any more complicated than it has to be; the trick is saving your fancy communication footwork for where it really counts—with your boss, in a meeting, or among the coworkers you work with on a regular basis. Otherwise, deal with challenging situations and styles directly and delicately, but don't say or do more than you have to. After all, our goal isn't to change anyone else (as if we could, anyway) or put ourselves or our careers in harm's way—it's only to use smart tactics to extract ourselves from situations that distract from our work or affect how we feel on the job. No, your challenging coworkers and their communication quirks aren't going anywhere, but arm yourself with a few choice phrases so that when you've got to handle something, you're ready.

If all else fails? "Kill them with kindness," says Lisa Lieberman, a senior-level hospital administrator at Memorial Sloan-Kettering Cancer Center. "I used to let difficult people at work drive me crazy, or play passive-aggressive games with them. For instance, if they weren't giving me information I needed, then I wouldn't give them the information they needed. Eventually, I realized I just had to be the bigger person. Now, when things like that come up, I simply say, 'It seems like you're not wanting to give me this piece of information.' I try to understand what's going on with them, and it totally throws them off guard. Needless to say, it works pretty well and I don't run into too many issues along these lines anymore."

Why One Size Does Not Fit All
When It Comes to Communication

What's the biggest communications gripe that managers of New Professionals share in common? "Informality," says Lisa Lieberman, a 15-year veteran at one of New York's largest medical centers. "I've noticed how some entry-level employees are extremely informal and overly relaxed in their verbal and written communications. I've read emails to senior-level people with no grammar or punctuation, where everything is written in lowercase letters with smiley faces. Your communication style shouldn't be stuffy or suffocating, but too much informality is unprofessional." Lisa Cerretani, a 28-year-old administrative manager in the same organization, agrees. "Some of the newer hires out of college will speak in the same style, manner, and tone with a surgeon as they would with one of their peers. But our surgeons here are highly experienced professionals and one of the most important groups of people in our organization, so the communication style we use with them has to reflect that."

Clearly, one size does not fit all when it comes to communication in the workplace, and tailoring your language, word choice, and emails for the appropriate audience is a must. Even tone of voice and body language may need to shift based on your audience, as one HR director pointed out: "You can't walk into the CEO's office and plop down in a chair. You need to be invited to sit, and when you do so, remember, you're not at home on the couch."

No matter how relaxed it is in your workplace, people probably care about communication more than you think, so don't necessarily assume that your coworkers are as comfortable with your informality as you are. While a senior-level employee or executive may not say to you directly "I prefer it when you punctuate your emails and leave out the smiley faces" (after all, they've got better things to do than correct your emails, right?), these folks have worked hard and earned the right to a little respect, and may not take kindly to your overly relaxed style or informality.

Finally, you might also find that an overly informal communication style will cost you career opportunities for leadership positions or greater visibility, even if you are doing great work. After all, your communication style reflects your understanding of your company culture and demonstrates an ability to connect with a diverse range of employees. If you can't write an appropriate email, would you really be taken seriously by employees if you were promoted, or by senior-level executives in a meeting where you were speaking? Pay extra attention to your communication style, so your message is always on target.

Handling Yourself Like a Pro: Strategies for Successful Communicators

No matter how easy or challenging we may find certain communication styles on the job, the real key to communication success rests with us. As we've stated earlier, we can't control what other people do or say, but we can do plenty to sound as good as we look. Try these pointers on for size to be the communicator everyone else admires.

- *PRACTICE PUBLIC SPEAKING. WHY:* Rehearsing your presentation, an upcoming meeting with a client, or when you ask your boss for a raise ahead of time (better yet, several times) is a no-brainer if you want to sound as smart as you really are in front of others and lessen feelings of nervousness or discomfort. When you rehearse,

rehearse out loud (better yet, in front of others, or record yourself)—talking through stuff in your head is fine, but it won't give you the same effect as really speaking. That's because things that look great on paper don't always sound as great when they leave your mouth, so practicing out loud ahead of time helps dètect where you need to change a word, a thought, or an idea to really make an impact. (Want to really get better? Join Toastmasters, the largest public-speaking organization in the world, with meetings and chapters located around the globe.)

However you choose to practice this skill, make sure it's one you work on and sharpen regularly. As Kevin Giglinto, VP of the Chicago Symphony Orchestra, puts it, "Often, being able to represent your department or being the person to deliver a presentation with results of work you have created is key to advancement. Public speaking is at the heart of a good deal of management and without that skill, it is hard to get promoted as you will eventually have to present to the board, other directors, investors, the press, or whomever."

- *LISTEN MORE. WHY:* Communication is a two-way street, so if you find yourself semi-listening to other people instead of focusing on them, you're only doing half your job. Many of us wind up rehearsing our own witty retort or brilliant response in our heads rather than actually listening to the person we're supposedly conversing with, or we simply jump in and interrupt, cut the other person off, or other-wise dominate the conversation. Not only is this behavior rude, but it also shows immaturity and impatience, and gives the message that deep down, it's really all about us. Use eye contact, gestures (nodding the head), and a zipped lip with the occasional "hmmm" to convey that you are truly listening and focusing on that other person.

- *WATCH FOR NONVERBAL COMMUNICATION BLUNDERS. WHY:* You could be sending unintended messages to your audiences with body language, gestures, and more. For example, poor eye contact (looking around the room or glancing down when talking) suggests a lack of confidence in you and what you're saying. Shifting back and forth on your feet, or leaning to one side when standing, also conveys a sense of discomfort and nervousness, so stand front and center and solidly on two feet when you speak. Sitting counts, too—ladies, don't sit like you're a guest on the Letterman show, with one leg tucked under the other—it looks young, too informal, and unprofessional. Two feet on the ground, legs crossed at the ankles, or a leg crossed over the other is fine—just don't swing your leg back and forth while you do it.

- *CORRECT OTHER NONVERBAL COMMUNICATION DISTRACTORS. WHY:* Even if you don't intend it, your meaningless or unconscious gestures could be sending the wrong message to others and distracting us from what you really intended to say. For example, crossing your arms at your chest is a defensive posture, and standing with hands clasped behind your back suggests that you're "hiding" something. Men, don't jingle change in your pockets when presenting in front of others—we focus on the change, not you. And, pretty please, no "fig leaf" gesture—the hands crossed in front of your crotch is the last thing anyone wants to see when you're giving a presentation.

- *WATCH YOUR LANGUAGE. WHY:* The words you use immediately impact those around you, so choose wisely. Like it or not, we are instantly impressed or unimpressed by someone's vocabulary, word choice, and vocal presence.

For example, speaking with an inflection ("My name is Elizabeth?") is a vocal blunder that is associated with women more than men, and conveys a lack of confidence in what one is saying. Using too much street-speak or slang is another no-no—people want you to sound educated and polished on the job and in front of clients. Bad grammar and bad words are another turnoff—use these at your own risk.

When it comes to communication in the workplace, there is plenty to say, whether it's about email and other written communication, dealing with challenging communicators, or simply discussing ways in which we can improve our own skills. There's so much to say because we're communicating all day long, from how we greet a coworker (or don't), to how we express ourselves in an email to a group of coworkers. In fact, even when we think we're not communicating, we're communicating, which is why it's so important to be aware of the nonverbal messages that we send out to others, too.

The good news about communication is that we do it all day, every day, so there is always ample opportunity to improve, fix what isn't working, and get better at this critical skill. After all, employers tell us that no skill is more important on the job, and nothing seems to impact our ability to get hired or promoted faster than our communication skills. At the end of the day, becoming a better communicator isn't a choice—it's a necessity in the workplace, and for the success of our careers.

UNSPOKEN RULE #5

Don't Network—
Build Relationships Instead

Learn How to Build Relationships On and Off the Job to

Ensure Lasting Career Success

Introduction:
When It Comes to Your Career, Nothing Matters More Than Networking

Networking is probably one of the toughest and most important aspects of our careers and overall professional development. Unfortunately, it's also one of the most hated, misunderstood, and, consequently, poorly practiced areas, which is probably why many of us dread networking altogether. Still, like it or not, we simply must do it. It's too competitive to land a future job, a promotion, or a new opportunity inside your company today without networking. Sure, there are probably some people who manage just fine on their own. But consider this: According to one online career Web site, nearly 700 résumés are submitted for a single job opening during a tough economy. Do you really want to compete against 699 other people every time you are going for an opportunity? Who can compete with those odds?

If you think that hard work alone will move you up the company ladder, think again. It's relationships—the ones you have with your manager, coworkers, clients, and more—that will get you there. You may have experienced this already—in fact, perhaps it was a friend or acquaintance who helped you land the job you've got today. But if you hate the idea of networking, it's time to accept the fact that meeting and greeting, making plenty of contacts and, hopefully, friends along the way, is also part of your job description. It may be tough at first if you're not used to this kind of thing, but like any of the strategies we've suggested in this book, the hardest step is the first one. Once you make networking a habit—and it must become a habit—you'll reap the benefits in ways big and small.

What Is Networking?

Networking isn't just about meeting people, or handing out your business card to anyone with a heartbeat. Instead, think of networking as having a deliberate system or approach for meeting the right people. Don't get the wrong idea: "Right" people doesn't mean meeting only those who have a certain pedigree or belong to the country club. Networking is about making contacts in a strategic, thoughtful manner, where you create connections with people who can help you in some way—and whom you can also help. For your purposes, this definition means that networking will probably extend beyond the people you already know, though this is always a great place to start. However, in many cases, you will have to go beyond your immediate circle of friends and family to really reap the rewards of networking . . . and that's where the trouble begins.

Step #1:
Break Your Bad Networking Habits: Avoid Common Blunders and Stay Smart

When it comes to networking, there is good, there is bad, and then there is just plain incompetent. It's no surprise to find many articles in the media that declare networking passé, out-of-date, or yesterday's news, because networking often seems artificial and unsophisticated by today's more savvy job seekers and career-minded professionals. After all, some of the images we have of networking—where we call up someone we've never met to ask them for an informational interview or for coffee, for instance—seem forced, artificial, and just plain ineffective.

Worse, networking gets a bad rap because of the wide range of common networking blunders that many of us commit. To avoid some of these, make sure you stay on the right side of the law and make smart networking a habit.

Bad networking scenario #1

A student contacts an alumna from his business school and speaks to her about her company, a place where he'd really like to work. The alumna spends 20 minutes of her time over the phone with the student and tells him that, unfortunately, there are no open positions right now at her firm. The student, dejected, hangs up and eventually moves on to the next alumnus, never to be heard from again.

WHY THIS DOESN'T WORK: When you don't get what you want, the answer is not to hang up the phone and fall off the face of the planet. After all, things change all the time—just because there isn't a job available today doesn't mean there won't be one a few months from now. But how would this networker know that? The minute he didn't get what he wanted (a job lead), he was off to the next person.

A BETTER APPROACH: Send a handwritten or typed thank-you note (not just an email, in other words) and periodically stay on this person's radar screen so that if and when a job opportunity does come up that you're right for, you're still fresh in that person's mind. Plus, when you stay in touch with someone else, you demonstrate your commitment to the relationship, build trust, and show that you're not just in it for yourself. (For tips on how to do this, read on in this chapter.) Oh, and did we mention, send a thank-you note?

Bad networking scenario #2
An administrative assistant is unhappy in her current job and wants to leave her company. She emails a copy of her résumé with a note to a distant acquaintance at another organization, asking her if "any jobs are available."

WHY THIS DOESN'T WORK: Imagine if you met someone, and before you even had a first date, you were asking for a hand in marriage. Insane? I would say so, but for purposes of this chapter, it's just another example of asking for too much, too fast. Don't forward a résumé to someone else without being asked to do so first—it's too presumptuous and it's more information than they may want to have about you at this very early stage in your communication. After all, the person on the other end of the phone or email doesn't really know you yet. Think about it: If you were working at a company, would you automatically help someone you hardly knew get a job?

A BETTER APPROACH: Before you fire off a résumé, send a polite introductory email instead. Ask for a brief informational interview, phone call, or other opportunity to learn more about the other person. Then follow up. Don't worry: They know why you're calling, and if they want your résumé, they'll ask for it. Another point: If you are asking for help, make it easy on the other person by being as specific as possible about what you want. Asking if "any jobs" are available makes it sound like you aren't clear about who you are and what you want to do next. Don't make the other person have to think that stuff through for you; always have a clear goal in mind before you reach out to others.

Bad networking scenario #3

A new employee is eager to move up the company ladder and believes in the importance of building relationships. He develops a plan to email every senior manager and vice president in the company to see if they are available to speak, meet for coffee, or have lunch at their convenience.

WHY THIS DOESN'T WORK: Sometimes there really can be too much of a good thing. I admire networking as much as the next gal, but this guy has gone overboard. Recruiters call this sort of person a "serial networker," and this isn't a good thing. By trying to meet anyone and everyone, you appear unfocused, unstrategic, and a tad desperate—kind of like the job-seeker who applies to anything and everything out there. Plus, with that many people contacted, word will get around that you're sending lots of emails, and folks may start to wonder if you actually do any work during the day.

A BETTER APPROACH: You're not right for everyone, and everyone isn't right for you. Be smart about protecting your time by thinking long and hard about who it really makes sense for you to contact based on your career goals. Ask your manager for input here if you're not sure. Once you've narrowed down your choices, make a Top 10 list of people you'd like to meet and work your way through, slowly. Networking is part of your job, yes, but it isn't your entire job. Don't get so focused on it that you lose sight of what you are actually getting paid to do.

Bad networking scenario #4

An employee is extremely uncomfortable networking with her more senior colleagues at work, because she feels like she has nothing to offer in return. She avoids it altogether, and figures that she will network when she has more to bring to the table.

WHY THIS DOESN'T WORK: Part of our networking discomfort

stems from the fact that we're approaching people we often don't know very well and asking them for something without necessarily giving something in return. We think, "What could I possibly offer Mr. Manager or Ms. Big Shot Client? I'm just a lowly customer service rep." Break out of this mindset, because networking isn't begging or asking for a handout, and it's never a one-way street, no matter how low on the totem pole you sit. You're ready to network *now,* regardless of your current job title, and the sooner you start to view networking as a two-way road, the easier it will start to feel to you.

A BETTER APPROACH: Pick networking strategies that seem like fun, not work. Consider what Kate Abend, a 28-year-old employee at the Union of Concerned Scientists, did to meet more like-minded professionals in Washington, D.C. "My friends and I organize happy hours and holiday parties to bring together people working on a range of public-interest issues. Turnout is excellent, and attendees can sign up for a Listserv where our community shares information about upcoming events and job openings."

Kate also suggests organizing smaller events to help socialize with people you work with every day. "In the nonprofit world, many of us work with a range of groups to advance our campaigns. Holding a coalition lunch or happy hour after your next meeting will build deeper connections."

In Kate's case, her willingness to reach out and network in creative ways has delivered real benefits. "Networking makes me more effective in my current job. When I was just starting out, it also helped me determine which groups might be a good fit for me in the future. While job performance is the key to advancement, building relationships is also critical for landing the right job—it certainly helped me land the job I have now!"

Bad networking scenario #5

An employee reaches out to several more senior colleagues and other contacts (friends of her parents, mostly) to try to learn more about her profession. She contacts her network frequently via email and over the phone, spending anywhere between 30 and 60 minutes on a single phone call.

WHY THIS DOESN'T WORK: As a networker, you never want to run the risk of wearing out your network of contacts. If you contact people too often, or eat up too much of their time and energy, it won't be long before you become someone people want to avoid, rather than help.

A BETTER APPROACH: Set some firm guidelines with yourself about how often you reach out to your contacts so that you don't overburden them. If you're asking someone for a brief phone meeting, for example, promise your contact that the meeting won't take longer than 20 minutes of their time, and stick to your promise. If you're having a terrific conversation with someone and 20 minutes are up, interrupt yourself and say: "I'm really enjoying this conversation, but I did promise to keep this to 20 minutes, and I want to honor that commitment to you. I know how busy you must be." While you're at it, make sure you've got a broad, diverse set of contacts, so that you're not going to the same people over and over again.

Step #2:
Learn Why Building Relationships Is How Networking Really Works

Networking isn't rocket science, but as the above examples indicate, there is more to this practice than meets the eye. The best approach? Starting now, instead of networking, think of this as relationship-building and your new goal is to have as many conversations with as many people as possible. That's it. Unlike some networking, which ends once you've gotten what you want from the relationship (i.e., a job, a sale, or a promotion), having conversations will help you build real, genuine relationships. After all, building relationships for business purposes works in much the same fashion that your personal relationships do—they take time and effort to create, but they deliver far greater rewards to you. When you build relationships over the long term, you allow people to get to genuinely know you, like you, and want to help you. When you try to take a shortcut, you don't give people that opportunity.

When you build relationships to last, rather than one-off networking calls or meetings, you'll have a much greater chance of someone actually passing your résumé along to the right people, singing your praises at the next meeting, or really going to bat for you than you might have otherwise. And, quite frankly, by demonstrating your interest in someone else for the long haul, you also demonstrate that you're a nice person—something that goes a long way in today's world.

How Relationship-Building with Conversations Works: One Example

When we talk about building relationships by having plenty of conversations instead of networking, don't panic: I'm not suggesting you sit around with your hairdresser and shoot the breeze all day long or try to turn everyone into your next best friend. As we've said before, networking requires focus and strategic thinking—your goal isn't to meet anyone with a job title bigger than yours, for instance.

Before we dive into lots of details, let's take a high-level view of how having conversations works: Let's say you currently work in an accounting role, and you've discovered it isn't for you. Instead, you'd like to work in a recruiting function inside your company. Slowly and methodically, you might start to have conversations with people who place you one step closer to a recruiting role. You could reach out to the person or people who initially recruited you, for example. From there, you might ask to be referred to other recruiting professionals within the firm that they know, and so on. Along the way, you make a point of sending plenty of thank-you notes and staying on everyone's radar screen.

At the same time, you might join a professional association for the recruiting industry to meet more people and gather more contacts. You could take a class or two at a local university that gives you even more knowledge of the profession, while reaching out to alumni and professors who might know people in the industry, and so on. One conversation at a time, you can get closer and closer to someone who might actually be in a position to hire you, and in the meantime, you're developing a broad network of like-minded professionals and transforming yourself from an accountant to a recruiter. This process can work under a broad range of different circumstances—whether you are looking to be placed on a highly visible project, transition into a new department, or even have a different boss. The key is always about slowly building relationships over time in order to do so.

When it comes to relationship-building, as opposed to traditional, one-off networking, you've got to be in it to win it. In other words, these things take time, and genuine relationships don't happen overnight, so get ready to commit to this for the long term. Building relationships is the best career tool you've got, but don't put a rush order on this job. People will get to know and like you on their own schedules and time frames, so if you're looking to make a career transition, get a sale, or land a promotion in the eleventh hour, this isn't your strategy.

Step #3:
Build a Circle of Contacts by Having Conversation after Conversation

Before you begin the process of relationship-building and having strategic conversations with the right people, start at the very beginning. If you were taking a road trip somewhere, you wouldn't just hop in your car and start to drive, would you? Chances are that you'd have a final destination in mind, plus ideas about where you'd like to stop along the way. You'd have a map, you'd have supplies packed—in short, you'd think and prepare before you just hit the gas pedal.

The same is true for this process: Before you start picking up the phone or sending off emails, know what your career destination is, too. Where do you want to be five years from now, and what needs to happen along the way in order for you to get to your destination? Once you know where you are going in the short term and long term, you are in a much better position to focus your time and efforts when it comes to networking. As we saw in our accountant-recruiter example, knowing the final destination (landing the recruiter role) helps you to make smart, strategic stops along the way (having conversations with plenty of people, joining a professional association, taking classes).

Regardless of where you are going, be sure to use conversations as an opportunity to branch out. For instance, consider the situation faced by 23-year-old Tina Reejsinghani, an

assistant brand development manager for a consumer products company. When Tina started her job, she joined the company along with an entire class of younger new hires.
"Because there were so many of us starting at the same time,
it was easy to be lumped into the 'younger group' by everyone else and not be seen as an individual performer instead."
If you've joined a company as part of a larger incoming class
or group where most of you are around the same age, be sure
to build relationships outside of the group to broaden your
own circle and avoid being labeled.

Finally, use conversations to find mentors, role models,
and other successful people whom you can emulate as you
journey further into your own career. Over and over, successful professionals point to the mentor relationships
they've sought out as key ingredients to their own success.
Whether it's a supervisor, coworker, or successful professional you've crossed paths with, reach out to people to get
the secrets, inside scoop, great advice, and terrific insights
you and your career can benefit from.

Having Conversations:
Kissing Some Frogs to Find the Prince

When it comes to networking by conversation, you're inevitably going to kiss a few frogs before you find the prince.
In other words, you'll probably have a bunch of conversations that aren't necessarily producing results before you hit
the jackpot, but that's just par for the course, so don't get discouraged.

So, who exactly are you supposed to have these conversations with? The truth is that anyone is fair game when it
comes to networking. Your friends, family, and friends of
friends and family are always a great place to start if you're
feeling shy, and your current and former coworkers and

colleagues are another natural source of names and contacts for you. Once again, your goal isn't to speak to everyone in the world, but you don't want to rule anyone out, because you never know where the prince resides, so to speak.

If you're stuck and not sure where to begin in terms of having conversations, try the "onion" approach:

The layering principle: Think onions
When it comes to this style of "new" networking, think of an onion. Like the aromatic onion, your networking strategy works best when you peel back a layer at a time to get to the heart of what you're looking for. If you stop at the first layer, you may not get what you need, so part of this process means having conversations with people you don't necessarily know—yet.

A "layer" is really just a group of people in your world who share something in common—for instance, your "marketing coworkers" might be a layer. Your "alumni from college" might be another layer. As you peel back a layer at a time, you get farther away from what is very immediate and familiar to you while moving closer to the center—in other words, as you "work your layers," you'll start meeting more and more new and less familiar people along the way. Don't let meeting new people stop you from networking. Far too many people shy away from the practice because they just aren't comfortable reaching out to people they don't know. But I urge you: Don't skip this step. A stranger today might be a wealth of contacts or knowledge for you tomorrow, so don't stop peeling back your onion at the first or second layer.

What could your layers look like? Here is one example:

- *LAYER #1:* Tell friends, family, and friends of friends and family about your goals/objectives.

- *LAYER #2:* Reach out to coworkers, clients, and other current business associates to learn more about your industry and their work.

- *LAYER #3:* Reach out to alumni from undergraduate and graduate programs who work in fields that interest you.

- *LAYER #4:* Contact a former supervisor and old coworkers from your previous job to update them on what you've been doing since you last worked together.

. . . And so on.

If you're still stuck, check out a few more tips for gathering names of people:

- *TIP #1:* Speak with faculty from your alma mater—many professors have worked within their respective industries and have great contacts. Use this overlooked resource.

- *TIP #2:* Read journals, trade association information, and newspapers, and look for leaders, experts, or other people quoted or named, then contact these people and ask if they could elaborate on their comments or thoughts with you. Ask librarians for help in identifying good journals or other resources to target. They are another great (and often overlooked) resource for networkers.

- *TIP #3:* Join associations and/or attend conferences that target your industry or profession. Go to events in your local area, too, and meet speakers, attendees, sponsors, and more.

- *TIP #4:* Look around your company for ideas. Which employees organize large events or head up big efforts?

Target the "people magnets" whom everyone else seems to like, too.

- *TIP #5:* Look for the "friends" of your organization. What clients, suppliers, other organizations, or outside vendors that you work with closely support what you do? Reach out to these ancillary groups, too.

- *TIP #6:* As an alumnus from your college, chances are that you still have free (or reduced-cost) access to many services offered by the Career Management Center. Through them, you may be able to receive information about employers, recruiters, and more—not to mention get plenty of help on your résumé and interviewing skills, too.

IMPORTANT NOTE: Never hang up the phone or end a conversation *without asking your contact to refer you to their friends and colleagues first.* Whatever you do, don't skip this step, because this is a critical component to how networks are built. If you approach your layer system in this way, you'll (hopefully) be in the position of never having to make a cold call. Some of your calls may be lukewarm, but getting referrals ensures that you'll always have a connection between you and the next person you're reaching out to.

Step #4:
Break Down the Networking Process into Five Stages for Best Results

You and I can theorize about networking all day long, but at some point, you actually have to *do* it. Formulating goals, having objectives, and determining how to reach out to the

right people are all important steps when it comes to networking. But only networking is networking, so let's bite the
bullet and get started.

When it comes to networking, remember that your goal is
simple—have as many conversations with as many people
as possible. In order to accomplish this, try this simple five-
stage process:

The Gathering Stage: Gather lots of names of people with
   whom you'd like to speak (your layers).
The Emailing Stage: Email (or write a letter if you're unable
   to get an email address) each contact.
The Follow-up Stage: A week after sending your email, follow up with a phone call to arrange a phone or in-person
   meeting.
The Meeting Stage: Have a meeting with your contact—
   where you dazzle and impress.
The Thanking Stage: Send a thank-you note and follow up
   with the next steps.

The Gathering Stage

*Gather lots of names of people with whom you'd like to
speak.*
As you read earlier in this chapter, you've already got a few
ideas to get you started, and in an ideal world, you may already have a sense of whom you need to talk to in order to
accomplish your goal. For instance, you might need the name
of the on-campus recruiter, a marketing manager, the head of
sales, etc. If you're stuck, start by creating a "hit list"—what
companies, types of jobs, or industries do you want to target?
What departments, managers, or other coworkers would you
like to reach out to? If you know that you want a fund-raising

job within the academic world, you could probably list multiple universities in your area that fall into this category. Or you might have a long-term goal of working for your company's London office, so you'll want to start gathering names of people who are already there, for instance.

The Emailing Stage

Send an email (or write a letter if you're unable to get an email address) to each contact
Once you've gathered your list of names, it's time to reach out to each of your contacts. Whenever possible, I recommend emailing or writing your contact in advance, rather than using the phone, for this initial contact. Here's why:

1. Email is the most preferred and utilized method of business communication in the United States today. Inside a business setting, busy professionals are much likelier to read and respond to email than other forms of communication.

2. By sending an email before calling, you've set the stage for your call, introduced yourself to your contact, and given them an opportunity to warm up to the idea of speaking with you. A phone call may abruptly interrupt your contact in the middle of a busy project or catch him or her off guard, and you may not get his or her undivided attention, or any attention at all. And, more often than not, people don't even answer the phone when they don't recognize the caller's number.

3. Finally, if you tend to get nervous or tongue-tied, or even if you're a non–native English speaker, communicating

over the telephone can be challenging when reaching out to a new contact for the first time. By writing an email or letter first, you have a chance to put your best foot forward and prepare your ideas ahead of time.

Your introductory email or letter should be brief, professional, and, above all, polite. Remember, you are asking for someone's time—a valuable commodity! Whatever you decide to write, make sure you get across the point that you are asking for the opportunity to converse with them and learn more. That's it. Your own agenda—whether it's to ultimately land a job, a promotion, or anything else—should be kept on the back burner.

Sample Email to a Former Colleague

Dear John:

It's been several months since you left our company, and I understand that you've landed a great position at Bank X. That's terrific news, and I know they are lucky to have someone with your capabilities.

As you know from our time together, I've enjoyed working in an analyst role with increased responsibilities at our company. With strong skills in systems integration and project management, I'm passionate about learning more about finance and helping a financially driven team or department succeed.

I know how busy you must be, and am hoping you might be willing to share some of your own experiences as a senior-level finance professional with me in a brief phone conversation.

Please don't hesitate to reply directly to this email if there is a particular date/time that is most convenient for you to speak. Otherwise, I will plan to follow up with you directly next week to schedule a phone appointment.

Many thanks in advance for your time and efforts on my behalf, and I look forward to speaking with you.

Sincerely,

The Follow-up Stage

A week after sending your email, follow up with a phone call to arrange a meeting. Wait longer if you've sent out a letter.

Here is where the fun begins: Ideally, once you've sent out your email in the previous stage, you'll receive a wave of positive responses from your networkees and have your phone appointments set up in no time. But don't hold your breath.

WORDS TO LIVE BY: You may spend several days, weeks, even months on this stage. The fact is that people are busy, and you simply aren't their first priority. Don't take this personally or feel bad when your calls and emails don't get returned. It happens to the best of us!

But don't wait around for people to call you back. It's so easy to get discouraged when phone calls and emails aren't returned or given any response—we assume this means a rejection or that they aren't interested in us. The result? Too many of us throw in the towel and give up far too easily. Promise me you won't go down this road. Have patience, persist, and keep reaching out to people.

If they don't call you back

I know what you're thinking: *"What if I call and leave a message and they don't call back? Should I leave another message? How many messages can I leave before it becomes annoying?"*

The questions point out an important issue: There is a fine line between following up and stalking. If you're leaving multiple voice mails or sending too many emails, you've crossed the line. How much is too much? There isn't any set rule, but if you want to avoid restraining orders, I recommend being *gently persistent*. Gently persistent means leaving the occasional friendly email or voice mail without getting impatient or angry, or going overboard. When in doubt, practice the Golden Rule, and do unto your contacts as you would have them do unto you.

To demonstrate how the gently persistent model can help, here's a system that I use.

First things first

I will often leave a friendly voice mail following up from my email (or letter). If I don't get a response within two to three weeks, I will leave a second, friendly voice mail. (*Always* keep your messages friendly. If you sound annoyed or angry that you haven't had your call returned, it will never get returned.)

If they still don't call . . .

If I still haven't heard back after leaving two voice mails, I will send out a second *email* to the contact, which is similar to the first one, but may include an additional line or two:

"I'm sorry I've missed you at the office, and would welcome the opportunity to schedule a brief conversation over the phone at your convenience. I certainly understand that this may be a particularly busy time period for you at work.

If so, please don't hesitate to let me know when there is a better time to reach you, and I'll follow up."

Now, if you *still* get no response from this contact, don't take it personally, eat a gallon of ice cream over it, or assume that the contact won't speak with you. But, to keep your self-esteem and sanity intact, end the communication for the time being. Instead, keep a record in Outlook (or whatever scheduling system you use) of when you called and what the outcome was (for instance: "Contacted Jane Smith on 3/12 and 3/31 and left voice mails. Followed up with email on 4/15.").

Put a reminder in your calendar to send her another email in six weeks or so. In your follow-up email, you can politely reference your earlier communication, and "update" her on your progress. Once again, follow up with a phone call from this email. If you *still* don't get any kind of returned call or response, you can put this contact on the very back burner.

Your Timetable	
Week	**Action**
1	Send out introductory email. If no response, move to week 2.
2	Follow up with a phone call. If no response, move to week 3–4.
3–4	Follow up with a second phone call. If no response, move to week 5–6.
5–6	Send second email with "sorry I missed" phrasing. If no response, record contact history in contact management tool.
12	Send another email referencing earlier communication and updates.

Seems like a lot of work for one contact? Look at it this way: It's worth it if this contact can help you achieve an important goal or objective. Once you develop a system, you'll find that your calls and emails go much faster, too. Think of this process a little like being in sales—after all, you need lots of leads to make a single sale. The more contacts you reach out to and pursue at the same time, the sooner you'll achieve your goal. All it takes is one well-placed contact to make the difference—so keep persisting.

The Meeting Stage

Have a meeting (over the phone or in person) with your contact—where you dazzle and impress
Congratulations! You've worked your layers, you've made the calls, and now you've scheduled an appointment (either in person or over the phone) with your contact. Call this meeting an informational interview, a conversation, or simply a terrific opportunity, and dazzle the heck out of your contact. You and I know how hard you may have worked in order to land this meeting, so don't try to wing it. Plan, prepare, and show up ready to make the most of your time together.

- Above and beyond everything else, you are there to learn. Andrew Broderick, a 22-year-old valuation analyst at Equity Methods and a Stanford-bound MBA candidate, met with a variety of people to learn and "get ideas." At one stage, he had contacted the father of his brother's Little League friend to learn more about the real estate industry. The result of several friendly conversations and lunches was an internship for Andrew, who was unexpectedly offered the chance to work in real estate development by the executive. When you keep the focus on learning about them, you can benefit in all sorts of ways.

- Prepare by doing your homework first. Research the company and the professional history of your contact, if possible. (For example, where did she go to school? Where else did she work? What are her greatest professional accomplishments?)

- Study up on your contact's industry, her clients, whatever you think is relevant to her role inside her company. Prepare a list of questions ahead of time and keep them in front of you during your conversation.

A Note about Questions

As we know, this conversation isn't dominated by your agenda, but there's no reason why you can't ask a few questions that reinforce your own goals, too. Don't be afraid to let the contact know how they can help you, provided that you've "set the stage" appropriately. In other words, blurting out "Can you help me land a job?" during the first few minutes of a conversation is not what we have in mind.

Instead, if you are a job-seeker, you could ask:

"If you were looking for a job in this field today, what would be the top five companies you would pursue and why?"

"If you were interested in learning more about opportunities in this industry, what conferences or meetings would you attend? What associations would you join? What publications would you read?"

"If you were hiring a finance graduate today, what would be the three most important skills you'd look for?"

And so on. Just be sure to catch yourself when you ask me-centered questions as opposed to you-centered questions. For example:

ME-CENTERED QUESTION: Are you currently hiring?
YOU-CENTERED QUESTION: What are the characteristics that you look for when hiring entry-level finance professionals?

ME-CENTERED QUESTION: Are there any openings in our London bureau right now?
YOU-CENTERED QUESTION: How did you make the transition from working in our offices in New York to being transferred to London?

Be sure to ask you-centered questions throughout the interview—in doing so, it will provide you with some helpful information and reinforce your own goals and objectives in a slightly more subtle way.

- Write down a list of key talking points ahead of time that should guide your comments throughout the conversation. To do this, think about the *three most important ideas* you'd like to leave your contact with by the time your conversation is up. Your talking points help simplify your message and position you and your skills in the eyes of your contact.

- Even though this is not a job interview, you should be prepared to answer questions about your work history, your professional accomplishments, etc. This contact may be informally screening you for opportunities inside his organization or for a certain project or leadership role, so the more polished, prepared, and professional you can sound during the conversation, the better. Additionally, these conversations are excellent practice for your future job interviews, so the more you treat them as such, the better.

- If your meeting is in person, dress sharp. You've worked hard to get to this point, so don't blow it by showing up in the wrong stuff. You don't need to wear a pin-striped suit, but wear a jacket (men and women) and dress professionally.

- Whether your meeting is over the phone or in person, have a copy or two of an updated résumé handy. Even if you're not a job-seeker but are simply interested in learning more about a profession or a company, or just want to get to know someone better, having your résumé nearby helps keep you and your talking points on track. Plus, you never know—your contact may ask you for it and want to see a copy then and there.

- Remember, never end a conversation without asking for additional contact names as referrals. Simply asking something like: "Can you recommend two or three other colleagues of yours that I might speak with to further explore my interest in finance?" or "Do you know anyone at Bank Y that I might also speak with?" can do the trick.

The Art and Science of Networking: It Doesn't Always Work Perfectly

Keep in mind that networking is an art and a science. You can design spreadsheets, get organized, and have a systematic approach for meeting people, but at the end of the day, building relationships isn't a perfect process. Even when you've done things beautifully on your end, you may not get any closer to achieving your goal. So, if you've done everything right, and your contact didn't ask to see your résumé, didn't offer to put in a good word for you, or didn't help in any way, large or small, there could be a variety of reasons why. Here are a few possibilities:

1. His organization is currently downsizing and doesn't have any job openings.

2. He doesn't feel you're a good fit for his company, project, opportunity, etc. and is too polite, shy, or indifferent to tell you.

3. He isn't sure you have the necessary skills or other qualities to succeed inside his organization and isn't sure how to approach this with you.

4. He is fairly new to his role and doesn't feel he has the pull or contacts to forward your résumé or name to anyone.

5. He is extremely busy at work and simply doesn't have the time to help you any further.

6. It never occurred to him to ask how or if he might help you.

There can be a million different reasons why someone may or may not be able to assist you at a particular time, and they may not have anything to do with you. On the other hand, if it does have something to do with you, you'll want to try to find out so that you can fix what isn't working by asking a few key questions. For example, you could ask, "Based on what you know about my background, are there any areas in particular that you'd suggest I get more training in before I pursue a career in fund-raising?" Or you could ask: "Can you think of any reasons why someone with a background similar to mine wouldn't fit in at the London office?"

Keep questions polite and nonthreatening, and, whatever you do, don't make a contact feel uncomfortable or put him on the spot. Because most people will be far too polite (and far too uncomfortable) to say something like "You seem like a good guy, but I just don't think you'd do well here," it's important for you to pick up on hints, clues, or other signals your contact is politely trying to give you, so be sure to read between the lines.

The Thanking Stage

Send a thank-you note
This is the easiest step in your relationship-building process, but it's often the most ignored. Don't forget to send a thank-you note, preferably handwritten (though typed is fine, too, if your handwriting isn't the best). If time is of the essence, it's fine to send an email thank-you, but emails often get buried in the clutter. Plus, it takes little effort to drop someone an email—a handwritten note goes a lot further in demonstrating your gratitude.

Regardless of how you do it, it must be done for a number of reasons:

1. First, it's the polite thing to do. Someone was kind enough to give you their time, and they deserve to be

thanked for that. You want to be thought of as someone smart, kind, and generous. Writing a note is part of building your own personal brand and reputation, too. Thank someone for a thoughtful email reply, a brief phone conversation—anything. Don't worry about overdoing it here.

2. Next, it differentiates you. Sadly, many people forget to thank others for their help and time or simply don't bother. The fact that you do will help you stand out in your contact's busy, crowded world.

3. It's also a smart thing to do. By writing a well-thought-out thank-you note, you are giving yourself the opportunity to get in front of your contact again. This is a terrific reminder to your contact of the conversation you had.

4. Finally—you never know what will come of it. I once obtained a highly competitive internship because I wrote a thank-you note to an alumna from my business school after she had a brief phone conversation with me. She later told me that she was frequently contacted by students and had never received a thank-you note except mine. The moral of the story: A little thank-you note goes a long way.

Want to Write a Thank-You Letter that Gets Remembered?

- *Be sincere*: Many of us take the time to customize a cover letter, but we often send the exact same thank-you note to everyone. The result? Your note sounds formulaic, rather than having a genuine, natural tone to it. Take the time to write a customized note that truly reflects your appreciation, and you'll impress the reader with your sincerity and honest thanks.

- *Be quick*: Don't wait too long to get that thank-you letter in the mail; aim to send a note within 24 hours (or a week at the most) of whatever it is you're thanking someone for. And while you're at it, drop the note in the mail. Sure, email is a quick way to say thanks, but a written letter tends to stand out and get noticed in ways that email doesn't. After all, how many emails do you receive a day versus thank-you letters in the mail?

- *Be legible*: To handwrite or not to handwrite? That is the question when it comes to thank-you notes, and the answer depends on whether we can actually read your handwriting or not. No doubt about it, a hand-written note always adds an elegant, personal touch to whatever you're writing, but at the end of the day, you want to make sure your note is read, so pick the medium that will make life easiest for your recipient.

- *Be thoughtful*: Don't be afraid to go the extra mile with a thank-you note when appropriate. If you find an interesting article or tidbit of information that is meaningful to your reader, include it with your note. I once sent a client some very funny Post-it notes that joked about something we had been discussing—it was a small gesture, and gave me another opportunity to thank her for her time in a fresh way.

- *Be smart*: Don't skip the small step of proofreading your note, particularly if you're sending out a few at a time. I once skipped this important step and wound up sending the wrong note to someone, which was embarrassing and undid all that good-will I had just created with my thanks. While you're at it, make sure to proofread what you've written and keep the typos and misspellings away.

Step #5:
Be the Gift that Keeps on Giving—Staying on the Radar Screen

In the beginning of this chapter, we said that networking isn't a one-time deal that ends once you've gotten what you wanted. If you're serious about building relationships, you can't vanish into thin air, never to be heard from or seen again once a thank-you note is written. When you network, you make the commitment to stick around for the long haul and stay in touch. Here's why:

- It's the polite thing to do. If a contact forwarded your ré-sumé to someone he or she knew, and you landed a job because of that action, you need to let your contact know. So many people are helped by others and never follow up to let their contacts know the outcome of their assistance.

- It's the smart thing to do. After all, if someone is willing to put in a good word for you today, there is no reason why they wouldn't put in a good word for you again down the road. In the example I shared earlier, I obtained an intern-ship with a thank-you note, but I eventually obtained two different jobs because I stayed in touch with this same contact. When you get in touch and keep in touch with people, all sorts of good things can happen.

- It's the right thing to do. When you stay in touch with someone, your actions show that your relationship really is a two-way street, and you're as committed to their suc-cess as they were to yours. Over time, you'll have the op-portunity to help your contacts out, give back to them, and reciprocate.

Don't Be Out of Sight, Out of Mind
When It Comes to Networking

In case I haven't beaten you over the head enough with this point yet, staying on someone's radar screen is part of the networking process. As I stated in an earlier example, just because someone doesn't have a job or opportunity for you today doesn't mean that they won't six months from now. When you keep in touch with someone, you stay at the top of their mind and will (hopefully) be the first person they think of when the right opportunity does come up. Staying on someone's radar screen is an absolutely essential technique that many professionals use—everyone from salespeople to job-seekers to plenty in between. Don't be here today, gone tomorrow; stick around for the long haul.

So, how exactly can you stay on someone's radar screen? Check out these tips:

- *TIP #1:* Remind people of your value by sending periodic emails (once every three months or so) to let them know if you've been promoted or achieved some other milestone. For example, if you recently landed a big client, received a glowing report from the vice president, or obtained a new degree or certification, let your network know: "John, I wanted to let you know that I recently completed my program in nonprofit management, and I'm looking forward to pursuing new opportunities in the field."

- *TIP #2:* Clip articles and send them to your network. Yes, it's a strategy employed by parents everywhere, but it's effective. Send a copy of the article and attach a note with a few updates. Emails work, too, but for the reasons I

stated earlier, hard copy often gets noticed (and appreciated) before emails do.

- *TIP #3:* Send business or other relevant books. Many people today employ this strategy as a twenty-first-century
  version of clipping articles. The truth is that it's easy to
  send books to just about anyone, and relatively inexpen-
  sive, too, plus books really show that you're thinking
  about that person on a whole new level.

- *TIP #4:* Offer research or other analysis that you conduct.
  This provides a double whammy: Not only do you add
  value to sending someone helpful information, but you
  showcase your abilities by demonstrating the kind of
  work you can do. For example, one woman who wanted
  to work at a consumer products company went to a gro-
  cery store and interviewed customers of the company's
  products. She then compiled her research and sent it to
  her contact.

- *TIP #5:* Send holiday cards (try unique holidays, like
  Thanksgiving or Fourth of July cards), birthday cards,
  even small gifts. You don't have to do anything extrava-
  gant here, but imagine the reaction on a contact's face
  when he receives a birthday card from you. Now, that's
  the kind of thing that will definitely keep you fresh in
  someone's mind.

- *TIP #6:* Invite your contacts to events, conferences, seminars, or other programs of interest. If you know an interesting speaker is coming to town, why not invite
  someone in your network to see her with you? I've heard
  of folks who invite people to work out, visit museums, or

see sporting events together, so depending on the level of your relationship, several options can work here.

There are dozens of ways to keep in touch with people, some more involved and elaborate than others. Pick and choose the methods that work best and feel most natural, and don't feel obligated to do this with everyone—focus on the princes, not the frogs. After all, you don't have the time to keep up with everyone, and you'll always want to save some effort and energy for the new people you'll be meeting along the way. Most important, keep your efforts consistent. Remember, don't worry about networking perfectly—just do something, and keep it up. Over time, you'll get a good sense of who belongs in your network and who doesn't, and you'll want to do your best for those who are doing their best for you.

UNSPOKEN RULE #6

Your Boss Holds the Keys to the Kingdom

Do What It Takes to Build the Relationship that Matters Most to Your Career

Introduction

Find me someone who has ever held a job, and I'll find you someone who's hated his boss. Call it karma, feng shui, or just the way of the world, but everyone seems to have had a boss they've disliked. Really disliked. Even bosses have hated their bosses.

Why the hate? For starters, as you've read thus far, the little things can get in the way of love. I, for one, find it hard to love the boss who clips his toenails in his office, as was the case with boss #3. Call me crazy, but I still harbor the slightest bit of ill will for the supervisor who returned a draft of a memo I had been working on with "I don't get this" written in large red letters across the top.

Despite these cruel injustices, it doesn't serve me—or you, dear reader—very well to sit around, be cranky, and stew in our own juices. Hopefully, you're working with a manager or supervisor who is enlightened and a joy to be around, or maybe your new boss is less than perfect. Perhaps you don't have a boss yet, but want to make sure you start off on the right foot when you do. Whatever the case, this is going to be one of the most important work relationships you'll have, and you'll want to do everything you can to make this relationship work. It doesn't mean you two have to be best friends, but like it or not, your boss holds the keys to your career, at least for the time being. Unless you want to ride shotgun for the rest of the trip, it's time to figure out how to love the one you're with.

Step #1:
Get to Know Each Other . . . the Right Way

What's the first step to building a great relationship with a boss, manager, or supervisor? Scan any one of the career guides at your local bookstore, and most send the same message when it comes to the employee-boss relationship: "Figure out what makes your boss tick," they tell us. "Learn what his expectations are," they suggest. Seems logical—after all, by getting to know our boss and understanding his needs from the beginning, we're in a far better position to deliver the goods, right?

Yes . . . and no.

Nobody is going to argue with the fact that in most cases, the more you know about your manager, the better. Naturally, there are some glaring exceptions to this general rule—I could have lived without the details of my boss's workplace pedicure habits, for instance—but generally speaking, forewarned is forearmed. Whether it's learning that your boss prefers email to voice mail or early morning meetings to late afternoon sessions, knowing and understanding her little quirks—and big ones—is all part of succeeding at work.

With that said, proceed with caution before you put all of your eggs into the information-gathering basket when it comes to building a strong foundation with your boss. You may have more information about the boss than the CIA, but at the end of the day, your relationship's success is really based on your ability to do a great job in whatever area you've been hired for. Because the first days, weeks, and months on the job are so critical to forming your workplace reputation and for paving the road with your boss, use the following tips to really start your relationship off on the right foot.

Tip #1: Don't push the panic button if you don't "click" with the boss right away

How long does it really take to build a relationship with someone? For most of us, our strongest relationships with friends, family, and significant others took months, or even years, to build. So why do we expect our relationship with the boss—one of the most important relationships we have on the job—to be any different?

THE SOLUTION: The truth is that it may not be love at first sight for you and your boss. Rather than worry too much about this, remind yourself that your relationship with your boss is a *relationship* and things take time to unfold and be revealed. For instance, you may come to find out that your boss's seeming unfriendliness is actually shyness, or that she wants to see how you perform on the job for a while before she really warms up to you. So instead of walking into a situation thinking that your boss will adore you right away, or even throw you a smile or two, accept the fact that it may not happen that way. The bottom line is that there is so much about your relationship that isn't known yet, and, in the meantime, you'll want to proceed slowly.

Tip #2: When it comes to learning about your boss, listening and observing is key

As you just read, you can't put a rush order on building a relationship with the boss. The same is true for the way you gather information. The reality is that most bosses want employees who are problem-solvers—people who are able to figure out stuff on their own without a lot of hand-holding.

So even if you've got the best of intentions, don't pepper your boss with a thousand questions during the first weeks at work. When you do, you run the risk of appearing insecure or overly needy, and, chances are, you won't have enough knowledge about your job yet to know what the answers to all your questions really mean, anyway.

THE SOLUTION: When you do all the asking, you may not be doing as much listening and observing—two skills that will serve you far better, anyway. By asking less and listening more, you'll gather much more valuable information. Not only will you get the answer to your questions, but you'll also begin to see how your boss approaches problems, offers solutions, and provides help. When you gather information slowly and steadily, it's like drinking from a glass, not a fire hydrant, and you'll wind up learning in manageable stages that don't overwhelm you or your boss.

Boss Hints!
Top 10 Things to Listen and
Observe from the Boss

1. Observe when your boss arrives and leaves each day—and then do her one better, by arriving earlier and leaving later. **Why:** Not only does it show your work ethic, but it also reinforces the fact that you're "part of the team" and are willing to contribute 100 percent to its success.

2. Listen for how your boss interacts with his boss. Is their relationship formal and buttoned-up or casual and relaxed? Do they meet and communicate frequently? Do they get along? **Why:** Seize the oppor-

tunity to study how someone with more experience than you manages their manager. Plus, learn how much respect your boss commands from his superiors, too—it can give you some good insight into how much he really accomplishes on the job.

3. Observe when your boss seems stressed and busy—and when he's calm and relaxed. **Why:** Learning when to approach your boss is key to getting your work done. Asking for him to sign off on something when he's up to his eyeballs in work may land you a glare or two, or worse.

4. Listen for the hassles and pain in your boss's day. **Why:** Figuring out what really challenges your boss on a daily basis—and how you can help take away some of that—will win you major points as a problem-solver. Whether your boss never finds the time to fill out her expense reports, or simply hasn't found a good system for handling clients' complaints, offer to help in that area. Even if she doesn't go with your plan, she'll appreciate the fact that you went the extra mile to make her life easier. Not sure where the pain is? Ask. Try: "Is there anything that I can do to make your day easier?"

5. Observe your boss's dress style. **Why:** Your mother said it long before we did: Dress for the job you want, not the job you have. Plus, when you don't look the part, it makes your boss look like he hasn't done his job and told you what's what. Do him a favor and look professional.

6. Listen for how your boss gives and receives information. Does she prefer detailed updates or brief sound bites? Does she want to hear from you once a day, or once a week? When does she prefer voice mail, personal contact, or email? **Why:** Give her information when and how she likes it, and chances are your requests won't get ignored. Plus, it lets your boss see that you understand which methods and styles of communication are most effective for getting the job done.

7. Observe your boss's work relationships around the office. Who else does she collaborate with besides you? **Why:** If your boss isn't around or is too busy to help, find out whether you can contact people within her network for further assistance. Getting help from other folks in the office takes some of the pressure off your boss, and allows you to broaden your network and exposure to others, too. Plus, you won't always have to wait around for your boss in order to get your work done.

8. Listen for your boss's pet peeves, complaints, and irritants. Does he hate to be reminded more than once about something? Is he driven crazy by long meetings? **Why:** Your boss is counting on you to make life easier, not harder. Start your own "what bugs the boss" list—figure out what drives him bonkers, then avoid it like the plague. Use your know-how to be a watchdog—if you know that someone wants him to participate in a long, boring meeting, warn him in advance what he's in for.

9. Observe what excites and energizes your boss. What gets him jazzed up? What is he proudest of? **Why:** When people share in each other's passions and joy, real connections can happen. If your boss has a deep interest in a cutting-edge software tool, why not dig around? Do some research about the software, find some articles, learn something interesting—and pass on what you've learned to your boss. Showing you care in small ways can pay huge dividends down the road.

10. Listen for your boss's own concerns and fears. **Why:** This may be one of the toughest things to figure out in any relationship, but press ahead. Even if your boss would rather die than admit it, he may wonder if he really is a good boss. Or maybe he worries about his kids and being able to spend enough time with them. Sometimes a simple comment ("John, I just wanted to let you know what a great mentor you've been to me") or gesture ("Let me finish that up for you. I know you don't want to be late to your son's soccer game") makes the biggest difference of all.

Tip #3: Remember, your boss is getting to know you, too
As you begin to develop a relationship with your boss, re-member that it takes two to tango. Your relationship isn't only about you getting to know her—she is also getting to know you during these first weeks. From how you dress to what time you show up at work, rest assured that the boss is slowly getting an impression of you and is assessing the ex-tent to which she can rely on you to get the job done.

THE SOLUTION: Help the boss get to know you . . . the right way. Because you're both still fairly unknown to each other, resist the temptation to overshare or offer too many personal tidbits of information in an attempt to generate a sense of closeness or friendliness. Trust me, it doesn't work—no amount of information sharing can force a relationship to develop any faster than it's meant to, and, in the meantime, you may wind up saying things that backfire or cast you in the wrong light.

For instance, consider a supervisor I'll call Jane, who is extremely focused, driven, and serious about getting the job done. Because she also happens to be young, fun, and friendly, some of her new hires have (wrongly) assumed that Jane is their "buddy" from day one, and tend to reveal a lot more than they should. Says Jane, "During his first few days on the job here, one new hire told me about how much he partied in college. I have no idea why he would share this with me—I think he forgot that I was his boss. Needless to say, it took me a long time to have any respect for him. The bottom line was that none of us took him too seriously, including me."

Even if your boss is the nicest gal in the world, be careful what you share about yourself, particularly in the beginning. You don't want to get a particular image of yourself ingrained in your boss's head. As time goes on, you may know it's perfectly OK to talk about a whole range of things. In the meantime, be friendly, stick to the basics, and remember that in these early stages, your new boss only needs to know three things about you:

1. You're ready to contribute and work hard for the team.

2. You appreciate the opportunity to learn from her.

3. You want him to know that you're here to make his life easier.

Resist the urge to share too many personal details or anything else that deviates too far from the three points above with your new boss. By keeping things friendly but professional, you'll be doing everything in your power to ensure a strong relationship down the road.

Tip #4: Remember that information is only as good as its source
There's an expression that says "Don't believe everything you read." When it comes to getting to know your boss, don't believe everything she tells you, either. This isn't to say that your boss is lying to you, but only to suggest that sometimes we say what we wish to be true, rather than what is. Consider the boss who tells his new employee, "My door is always open," then keeps his door closed for half the day. Or the boss who says, "I am here to help you," but then takes two weeks to reply to any of the emails you sent requesting assistance.

THE SOLUTION: We're not suggesting that you become cynical, assume that your boss is lying to you through his teeth, and forget the whole relationship thing. Instead, consider that you may or may not be getting the full story when your boss answers your questions and offers information. For starters, your supervisor, for confidentiality reasons, may not be able to share certain things with you. Maybe he's got his own history, frustrations, or other issues going on inside the workplace (don't we all?) that may skew his perception of reality.

And, finally, nobody wants to seem like a jerk, including your new boss. She does want to help, be available, and otherwise contribute to your success inside your organization—but she also may be too stretched, busy, or just too darn tired to do everything she's promised you. Just as you might read more than one newspaper for the news, consider the same approach at the office. Develop a range of relationships (see more in our networking chapter) so that your information comes from a variety of sources—not just from the boss.

At the end of the day, getting to know your new boss is a critical first step in your employee-boss relationship. Just remember that the information you receive may contain flaws or biases, and isn't any guarantee that you're going to become closer, faster. The bottom line: Be patient. Do what is in your power to get your relationship started off on the right foot, and then focus on your work. Excellence on the job is one factor that is likely to help just about any relationship with the boss, anyway.

Step #2:
Managing the Manager:
How to Survive Any Type of Boss

Over the first days, weeks, and months on the job, you've been gathering enough information on the boss to make the CIA look like child's play. Well done; by taking the time to figure out your boss's needs, pains, frustrations, and joys, you're laying the groundwork for a strong relationship with the boss—and for your future success on the job, too.

Yet for all of your hard spy work, you may or may not be thrilled with the results. After weeks and months of patiently gathering information, you're starting to get a crystal clear picture of what your boss is really like. And it may not be pretty. Perhaps, lucky you, you've got a boss you respect, and a boss who respects you, too. Maybe you have a boss who can really teach you about success from inside your organization, offering valuable training from someone who knows the ropes. And you've really won the good boss lottery if your manager appreciates you, challenges you, and values what you bring to the workplace—and doesn't mind singing your praises to others, either.

But what if your boss is less than perfect? Or is really, really less than perfect? Then what? The sad truth is that many people leave great jobs, good companies, and plenty of future opportunities simply because they weren't able to get along with the boss. Don't make this mistake. Nobody is suggesting you put up with an abusive or completely incompetent boss, but don't throw out the baby with the bathwater and walk away from a job you love simply because your boss is somewhat less than ideal. At the very least, think of it this way: Do you really want to give the boss the satisfaction?

In this day and age, with so many different managers changing roles, switching departments, or getting downsized, rightsized, and dumped, chances are that you won't have to put up with a bad boss for too long. To be fair, it can seem like an eternity when you are working for Attila the Hun, Cruella De Vil, or someone in between. Don't suffer alone: Read on to learn what you can do to survive any type of boss who comes your way.

The Micromanager

HOW TO SPOT HIM: It's not tough. He's the guy breathing down your neck, looking over your shoulder, and calling you every three minutes to check on how things are progressing with the report you're working on. Micromanagers have a hard time giving up control and have you on a very short leash. Plus, they drive you completely nuts.

HOW TO MANAGE THE MICROMANAGER: Consider his perspective—as your manager, his butt is on the line with everything you do. When you screw up, it's more work for him, and he isn't sure he can trust you to get things right. Perhaps he was burned in the past by a former employee and just isn't willing to take chances on letting you work solo. Or maybe he's a control freak who won't let go, or thinks nobody can do the job but him.

TRY THIS: Think of your Micromanager as a strict, over-protective mom who worries about everything and who feels much better when she knows exactly what is going on at all times. Send daily updates, weekly reports, detailed voice mails—whatever it takes to keep the boss very, very informed. If you smell the faintest whiff of a problem in the air, let your Micromanager know immediately. As Equity Methods president and CEO David Roberts (who is certainly not a Micromanager himself) puts it: "Never let a bump in the road become a pothole. Keep me informed."

If you want your Micromanager to give you more independence, start with something small to test the waters. Show the Micromanager the benefits of giving you some space and managing you less—for instance, he can save time, gain productivity, and strengthen your skills and abilities in the process. And remember, trust is earned. Don't expect your boss to let you handle the presentation or the proposal on your own for a while. No boss, no matter how relaxed, is handing over the keys to the Porsche until he's darn sure that you can really drive.

The Absentee Boss

HOW TO SPOT HER: Good luck. If you happen to catch a glimpse of her in the office, she's either running out the door to a meeting or is buried in a conference call. You see her so seldom, you hardly remember what she looks like. Often the

Absentee Boss leaves you wondering what you're supposed to do and how you're supposed to get it done.

MANAGE THE ABSENTEE BOSS: Why are some bosses so hard to get hold of? For the Absentee Boss, her disappearing act might be explained by the fact that she's being pulled in too many directions and doesn't have time for you right now. Or, let's face it, some managers simply don't want the job or responsibilities that come with managing someone, and it could be that she prefers handling the tasks of her job rather than managing you. Whatever the reason, that's little comfort to those of us who would actually like to see our boss once in a while, if only so they can see all of the great work we're actually doing.

TRY THIS: First, try like heck to get your boss to agree to a weekly meeting. Even if she'll only give you five minutes, force her to put something on her calendar each and every week (or more) that is exclusively time for you. Don't let her off the hook here—make sure you get a regular standing "date" with her, so that even if she's pulling a disappearing act the rest of the week, you know you'll have your regularly scheduled meeting to ask questions, get her to sign off on stuff, etc. Once you've got your meeting, run it like a tight ship—be extremely prepared, and keep your points short, sweet, and concise. If you aren't prepared or waste time, it will be that much harder for you to get her attention the next time you need it.

Dos and Don'ts
for Getting the Help You Need

Let's face it—many managers have a bit of the Absentee Boss in them. More often than not, we have to rely on emails and voice mails to the boss to ask our questions and put in requests for help . . . and then we sit back and wait . . . and wait . . . and wait . . . for an answer. If you've struggled with getting your boss to answer your questions and give you the help you need to get the job done, consider the following Dos and Don'ts.

DO *ASK YOUR QUESTION . . . THEN MOVE ON.* Most employers want employees who don't need tons of supervision and who can really take the ball and run with it on their own. This can seem scary, particularly when we're asked to do something we're not sure about. But the reality is that your boss just doesn't have the time to tell you exactly what you need to do—that's a huge drain on energy, productivity, and resources that he or she just doesn't have.

DO *PUT REAL TIME AND EFFORT INTO DEVELOPING OTHER RELATIONSHIPS AROUND THE OFFICE.* By broadening your circle of contacts, you'll have other people to turn to for asking questions, getting help, and simply learning more about the company. Plus, you'll give other people besides your boss a chance to see your terrific self in action—something important when it comes to future opportunities and promotions.

DON'T *DRIVE YOUR BOSS CRAZY UNTIL HE OR SHE HAS THE TIME TO ANSWER YOUR PLEAS FOR HELP.* When you send your boss too many emails and voice mails "reminding" him about your issue, you run the risk of quickly become annoying and looking desperate. You send the message that you expect your boss to hold your hand, but bosses expect you to take initiative.

DON'T *STAND OUTSIDE YOUR BOSS'S DOOR,* waiting for her to get off the phone so you can quickly get your question in. This tends to really drive people nuts—after all, your boss may not want you listening in on her calls, she may not want to be interrupted by you, and she will get back to you when she's ready. Plus, don't you have better things to do than stand outside her door all day?

The Slave Driver

HOW TO SPOT HIM: Easy—he's the boss who likes to schedule meetings on a Saturday afternoon, who wants to review your memo at 7:00 on a Monday morning, and doesn't seem to bat an eye about calling you on your vacation to discuss an upcoming project. Hardworking? Sure, but the Slave Driver takes it to a scary new level, where it seems there is little else that matters to him more than work—and you're expected to follow suit.

MANAGE THE SLAVE DRIVER: Managing the Slave Driver is tricky—after all, if he is your boss, you can't very well say no to the early meetings, the Saturday work sessions, or anything else for that matter, can you? The answer is . . . maybe.

How to know? Start by taking a look around the office: Do you work in a company that celebrates a "work hard/type A personality" type of culture? Have you noticed that many of your colleagues work weekends, come in early, or stay late? If that's the case, accept the fact that you're part of a company or industry where working long hours is par for the course and your Slave Driver boss is simply one of many around the office. On the other hand, if you and your boss are usually the only ones burning the midnight oil, you may have some room to negotiate.

TRY THIS: If you've truly got a Slave Driver on your hands, you owe it to yourself to take a stand. Still, tread very, very carefully when telling your boss no in any way, shape, or form. Even if your boss is being unreasonable, you're still the new kid on the block, and the last thing you want to do is gain the reputation of being unreliable, being lazy, or not holding up your end of things. Before you say something you'll regret, consider some of the pointers in the box below.

How to Say No without Saying No

• Let your boss know how much you care about getting the job done—and how much you value working "smart" instead of just working "hard." When you're not under pressure or a big deadline, sit down with your boss and say something like "John, I've noticed how much extra time we put in on weekends and evenings to get the job done. Would you be open to having me come up with a few alternatives to how I can complete my work in a shorter time frame?" Remember, you're not criticizing his management style, you're simply offering a couple of creative ideas for improving your process or work flow.

• Ask the boss to prioritize. If he's putting so much on your plate that you're practically forced to come in each weekend just to keep from drowning, try: "Realistically, John, I've been working long hours to complete this, but I just don't know if I will be able to complete everything before the end of the week. What is the most important thing you'd like me to finish before I leave the office?"

• Do you need more help? Perhaps the Slave Driver needs this pointed out to him, tactfully. Try: "John, are there any plans in the works to hire anyone else for the team? I've noticed that we're usually the only ones working weekends—maybe we could use an extra pair of hands."

• Appeal to his softer side. Try: "John, I realize how important this is to you, and believe me, I also want to get this done right. However, I usually spend my weekends with my family—would you be comfortable if I held off on this until Monday?"

• Avoid saying the actual word "no," even if it's what you mean. "No" is a loaded word—it's strong, it's finite, it closes the door, and it can sound disrespectful when aimed at the boss. So instead of saying "No, I won't come in and work this Saturday," try "John, I care about this job, and I'd like to work out a different arrangement with you, if possible. Is there any reason why this can't wait until Monday?" Feeling brave? Try: "John, is there any pressing reason why this can't wait until Monday so that I can keep my weekends free?"

Keep in mind that there are always situations that require more of your time and energy, no matter what the job, and many of us put in longer hours at various times throughout our careers, including early on. This isn't only because we're sometimes expected to "pay our dues" as newer employees, but also because it takes time—sometimes, lots of time—to figure out how to really do our jobs well. After all, if you're new, you're *new*—of course it will take extra hours to understand what's what. As New Professionals, it may be a very smart move to put in more time than everyone else, Slave Driver boss or not.

"Dear Liz"

More Managing the Manager: Answers to Some Tough Boss Situations

Whether you're working for the Micromanager, the Absentee Boss, or the Slave Driver, know that you're not alone. Because these bosses embody the types of characteristics that baffle, bewilder, or frustrate the heck out of many a New Professional, we've devoted ample time to each, as you've just read. Nonetheless, we know we haven't even touched the tip of the boss iceberg. If you've got a puzzling boss situation on your hands, ask Liz for help! Read on for her answers to our toughest boss questions.

Dear Liz:

My boss is an idiot! He never graduated from high school, uses poor grammar, and can barely spell. Plus, he tends to push products on our customers that they really don't need, and seems kind of shady. I just have no respect for the guy. Problem is, he's a top seller in the company, so nobody can touch him. What should I do?
Sincerely,
Working for Bozo

Dear Working for Bozo:

Sounds like a classic case of "take what you want, leave the rest behind." While nobody is suggesting you emulate your boss's somewhat ethically challenged practices, it sounds like he's got a thing or two to teach about sales and success. Respect that he's succeeded in spite of the fact that he may not have had the money or opportunity to continue his education. Instead of dismissing him, figure out what he learned from the school of hard knocks. Take him to coffee, ask him questions, observe him on client calls or meetings. Learn what's worked so well for him and leave what you don't like at the door.

Dear Liz:

My boss is a nice guy, but seems scatterbrained and all over the place. He's got big-picture ideas and then sends me off to execute—but seems to have no clue about what's really involved. For example, he asked me to "revamp our computer system" once (I'm his assistant)—a huge job! He just seems a bit clueless and disorganized. Help!

Sincerely,
Working for Scatterbrain

Dear Working for Scatterbrain:

Rather than get nervous when your boss asks you to take the ball and run with it (even if it seems like he has absolutely no idea what the ball is or where he wants it to go), think of this as an opportunity for you to step up, take charge, and show what you're really capable of.

Still, before you run off in ten different directions,

don't make a move until you and the boss have agreed on some kind of time frame, process, or system for approaching whatever he wants done to make sure the project is really doable, affordable, realistic, and so on. Even if you have to sit down with the boss, put the pen in his hand yourself, and force him to write, do what you can to get him to spell out exactly what results or goals he has for the project in writing first.

Dear Liz:

My boss is bad news. She takes credit for work I do, and never seems to do anything herself. She's worked for the company for over 15 years and just keeps getting promoted. I can't figure it out.

Sincerely,

Working for the Bad News Boss

Dear Working for the Bad News Boss:

While it may seem completely wrong and unfair to think of someone else taking credit for your ideas, working for a boss who does so may not be the career disaster you think, says Valerie Louzonis, a former fashion industry executive at a major jeans and sportswear company, who worked for over 25 years in design, manufacturing, and merchandising roles. Says Louzonis, "Fashion is a creative process, and it wouldn't be unusual to find yourself sitting in a meeting and hear your boss present ideas that you came up with as if they were her own." When this happens, here's what not to do: Get outraged, indignant, and go over your boss's head by telling the powers that be (or anyone else who will listen) that *you* were the one who came up with the brilliant idea. "Going around telling everyone that the idea your boss presented was really yours only makes you look immature and un-professional," says Louzonis. "Chances are that every-one already knows the kind of work your boss is capable of, particularly her own boss, so don't be sur-prised if people really know that you were the one who came up with the ideas, anyway. Plus, if you work for a boss, then, technically, the work that you do belongs to the company and your department any-way, so don't get too hung up on who did what."

What to do instead? Keep on producing good ideas, suggests Louzonis, and adopt the attitude that if an idea or two doesn't get attached to you, you'll still ben-efit in the long run. "After all, if your boss thinks highly enough of your work to take credit for it as her own, you're probably doing good work in the first place," she adds. Finally, keep in mind that bosses come and go. "If you're working for a bad one now, that could change, and you don't want to hurt your career in the meantime," advises Louzonis.

On the other hand, if you're genuinely concerned that your career is suffering because of your boss's an-tics, think like a lawyer. First, gather witnesses: Whenever you work on stuff, make sure that other peo-ple (besides your boss) are in the loop as often as you can. Also, gather evidence: Keep a running report (on-line and hard copy) of everything you've been working on, so that you have a paper trail of your efforts.

Dear Liz:

I feel like I'm being punished for doing a great job. Because I strive to do my best and go the extra mile, my boss always comes to me first for everything. At first I was flattered, but now it seems that every assignment gets dumped on me, and my lazier coworkers are living on Easy Street—meanwhile, we all have the same titles and salaries! How do I get ahead without having everything land on my plate?

Sincerely,

Drowning in Work

Dear Drowning:

Forgive me, but your letter reminded me of the times when I used to complain to my parents about having to do more chores than my brother, or sister, or friends from school, or whoever. Their response? "Life isn't fair."

I'm not suggesting that you don't have a legitimate gripe, but you seem to have the mind-set that we're all on equal footing at work and, therefore, should share equally in the workload. I beg to differ. The reality is that people have talents in different areas, and even if you and your coworkers do share the same title (are you sure about salaries?), your boss clearly holds you in higher esteem and feels that he can count on you to handle more than some of your peers. Don't assume that you won't get rewarded for this the next time a bigger bonus or promotion comes around; better yet, do a great job at whatever the boss throws your way, and continue to outshine the rest of 'em.

Having said that, you don't want to get dumped on with every assignment that your other coworkers have avoided. The next time you feel like everything has landed on your plate, approach your boss and ask, *"Would you consider assigning someone else on the team to share this project with me? I've got several other things I'm working on for you right now, and I'm concerned that this won't get done on time."* You could also ask for the assignment to be given outright to someone else, and you'll "supervise" the efforts.

Step #3:
Manage Yourself: Be the Kind of Employee Bosses Love

When it comes to having a great relationship with the boss, think of another line from the movie *Jerry Maguire,* when Tom Cruise, who plays the sports agent Jerry Maguire, yells to his client, a football player: "Help me help you! Help me help you!"

As strange as it may sound, you've got to help your boss help you when it comes to your success at work. Don't assume that just because your boss is your boss, he's going to want to go the extra mile for you when it comes to helping you in your career. Think about it: Would you spend your free time and energy on someone who didn't really deserve it? Your boss is the same way. Become the type of employee that your boss will be dying to help out however he can. Where to start? Read on.

Four Rules to Employee Success: How to Help the Boss Help You

Rule #1: Gain the boss's respect
Want your boss to really go to bat for you? Gain his respect. Sure, it's nice if we actually like each other, too, but respect is really what we're going for here, and our ability to get it from the big cheese boils down to one thing: professionalism. And what does it mean to be a professional? In a nutshell, it boils down to one simple concept: "You can count on me."

Everybody—especially your boss—wants to be able to count on you. He really does want to trust you, to rely upon you, and to know that you are there to work hard and contribute because it makes his job easier in countless ways. And you want to earn that trust, because once you've got it, you'll be given greater responsibilities—which means more opportunities, visibility, and career success for you. But you won't get any of it if your boss can't count on you.

Rule #2: Know what really matters to your boss

Here's the dirty little secret about work: All along, you've been thinking that it's your ability to perform your job well that really counts. After all, that was certainly the case in college, where grades were awarded based on performance, not on whether or not we were nice people.

In some respects, the workplace is no different, in the sense that you are expected to learn certain tasks and to do them well. But the unspoken truth is that it's the other stuff—including your professionalism, attitude, maturity, ability to work with others, etc.—that really earns you the A. That's why someone who doesn't have your brains or abilities may get the promotion sooner than you—if they've got heaps of that je ne sais quoi and you don't. After all, if people find your attitude cocky, they just won't want to work with you, no matter how brilliant you are. And that makes it harder for you—and your boss—to deliver results.

Rule #3: Do the job you were hired for

Let's assume that you are professional. You are a nice guy. People really do like you. Here's where things can get frustrating: You think you deserve more responsibilities, less grunt work, bigger challenges because you've been performing the job so well. But your boss isn't biting. You keep getting the same stuff to do, week in, week out, with no end in sight, despite your subtle pleas for more interesting work. What's the deal?

The deal is that your boss isn't satisfied you're ready, to be blunt. You may have mastered the task-related aspects of your job brilliantly, but you still haven't really demonstrated the other, less tangible evidence of your professionalism, maturity, and so on. Read carefully: The key is to *demonstrate* what you've got. You may be as professional as they come, but let's face it, some bosses aren't the brightest bulbs in the place, and you may have to really hit them over the head with your professional ways. Or, to be fair, perhaps you haven't always put your best foot forward, or, more likely, your boss is simply too darn swamped and busy with her own work to notice if you had. If you really want to get ahead: "Put in 10 to 12 months of hard work and show the right work ethic, because managers today won't trust your work ethic out of the gate," according to a vice president at Charles Schwab, Dale Kalman. "The question to ask is 'What do I need to do to get to the next level?' not 'When am I getting to the next level?' "

Rule #4: Admit what you don't know
Inside the classroom, you're given ample opportunity to ask questions and get answers. In the working world, that's not always the case. Supervisors can be extremely busy and have deadlines of their own to manage, and may assign you work without giving you lots of guidance, as seen with the Absentee Boss.

Rather than ask for clarification or help, New Professionals can sometimes feel like their questions are excessive or dumb, or that they are simply being a bother to their bosses, so they clam up, deciding to just figure it out on their own. Now, there's nothing wrong with being a problem-solver, but if you've got questions, and didn't get a chance to ask them, you owe it to yourself to get the help you need to get the job done right. Don't try to be a hero and do it all on your own if you're stuck. After all, you're new and you've probably never done this kind of work before, so give yourself a break.

Master the Art of Asking Questions

- To ask or not to ask: That is really the question. Does this need to be asked in the first place? Respect your supervisor's time, and make sure you've done your homework first and exhausted other channels (reading through company information online, asking less-swamped peers for help, etc.) before you approach him or her.

- Next, be organized with your question. Have documents or handouts ready for your boss if you need to refer to them. Make questions short, sweet, and to the point. Long voice mails and wordy emails are unnecessary, time-consuming, and probably won't get read, anyway. Less is more.

- Finally (and most important), ask questions *and offer solutions* at the same time. Don't simply kick a ball into your supervisor's corner and expect her to do the thinking for you. It's up to you to show that you really have thought the issue through and done your thinking before approaching her.

Step #4:
Avoid the Mistakes that Hurt the Employee-Boss Relationship

Have you ever noticed how easy it is to ruin a good thing? If you've ever spilled coffee on a new shirt, added just a bit too much salt to a recipe, or thought that anchovies would make a great pizza topping (sorry, I hate anchovies), you've experienced the speed at which a good thing can become bad. In fact, this good-to-bad transition can happen so quickly, you're not even sure what happened—all you know is that you're staring at a large brown coffee stain and a shirt you'll never wear again.

Whether it's a big mistake or a small one, it's all too easy to let your relationship get off track with the boss. Fortunately, our bosses have made a mistake or two themselves along the way, and they're usually pretty forgiving of our gaffes. Still, forewarned is forearmed: There are some mistakes that you don't want to make on the job, forgiving boss or not. Read on to learn which to avoid, and why.

Mistake #1: Not Showing Patience and Humility

"Nothing is more annoying than when a new intern or hire out of college comes in . . . and immediately starts telling us about his 'great' ideas, or about how we can improve such-and-such a thing. Meanwhile, he's been working for a grand total of four months and really has no clue about how our business operates. It's just plain arrogant."

Ouch! Could this manager at a large accounting firm be talking about you? Consider the number of times that you have been given unsolicited advice, "helpful" opinions, or other ideas that you didn't ask for and didn't want, and that, quite frankly, aren't always so useful and helpful in the first place. Irritating, isn't it?

Does this mean that we shouldn't offer our ideas or suggestions for improvement to the boss? After all, isn't that why they hired us?

Well, actually, no, that probably wasn't why you were hired. In fact, you were probably hired to help the team run a few yards, rather than score the touchdown. You were hired to do your job, at least for the time being—not the job of your boss, the CEO, or anyone in between. And when people try to do that, even when they have the best intentions, it bugs the folks at work. Especially your boss.

This isn't to suggest that your efforts, initiative, and go-getter attitude aren't appreciated. In fact, New Professionals are hired precisely because organizations love their energy, enthusiasm, and fresh approach to work . . . but organizations also tend to reward humility, patience, and a respect for their process, no matter how slow, annoying, or just plain wrong you think their process might be.

Mistake #2: Feeling Entitled

What really bugs managers of New Professionals? Above and beyond everything else, it's the feeling of entitlement that many new employees walk in with. Not sure if this could be you? Ask yourself the following questions.

- Do you think you deserve a raise, promotion, or more responsibilities *and* does your boss agree? Do you agree on the same time frame for your raise or promotion, or do you think it should happen sooner than your boss does?

- Do you often find yourself thinking, "They aren't letting me work to my full potential!" or "They aren't using my talents" at work?

- Did you try to negotiate your salary before you started your very first job out of college?

- Do you think you're smarter than your boss? What about other people you work with?

- Do you often find yourself interrupting or planning what you're going to say next inside your head while someone else is still talking?

- Did you find yourself gunning for your next promotion or raise shortly after you started your current job?

- Do you find yourself delivering ultimatums like "If I'm not able to do/get X, then I'm leaving"?

- Do you often wonder what you'll be getting (in terms of raise, promotion, more challenging work) in exchange for doing something above and beyond your job description?

- Do you find yourself wanting to quit a job within a couple of months of starting?

If you answered yes to most of the questions above, you may need to put the brakes on your expectations and get comfortable with the slower process in your workplace. This isn't to suggest that you don't deserve a promotion, for instance, but only that you consider that things on the job happen slower—often, much slower—than we think they should. Overnight success, instant celebrity, and other reality TV moments don't usually happen at work.

Help! I'm Surrounded by Idiots! Being "Smart" in the Office

Meet Adam, a 23-year-old customer service representative at a large financial services firm in New England who hates dealing with "stupid people" on the phone all day. "It's annoying to have to explain the same things over and over to customers," he complains. What about Alison, a 26-year-old computer programmer who doesn't respect her boss? "I have no respect for people who aren't smart, and my boss isn't smart," she says. Most of us have a healthy respect for others, but if you find yourself secretly thinking everyone else is an idiot, think again.

"Needing to be right says more about you than your boss or clients," says Rebecca Tate, a 32-year-old lead quality analyst for a financial consulting firm. "The products we sell are extremely complex, and I work with some very bright people. But if your clients can't understand you, that's about you, not them." Her suggestion? "Don't struggle to be right all the time. Give people a chance and hear them out."

Finally, those who aspire to move up in an organization need to overcome the belief that they are smarter than everyone else, including their boss, says Lisa Cerretani, a 28-year-old administrative manager at Memorial Sloan-Kettering Cancer Center. "It seems like no matter where you are inside an organization, the tendency is to think that you're smarter than your boss. But it's because of that thinking that you are in the role you're in." She adds, "So much goes on behind closed doors, and you really don't know what goes into the decision making, so what might seem like the obvious answer to you may be more complex than you realize." And let's face it: People who point out how much smarter they are than everyone else just wind up looking stupid in the process.

Mistake #3: Lacking Confidence and Courage

Are you confused yet? We've been saying, over and over, how important it is to eat a bit of humble pie from time to time . . . and now we're suggesting that a lack of confidence is a no-no on the job? What's the deal?

If you've ever wondered why the bozo three cubes down from you just landed the juicy promotion that you were convinced you deserved but didn't snag yourself, you may want to do a quick confidence comparison and find out whether bozo comes out ahead. Over and over, studies show that those of us who are able to convey our own confidence and belief in our abilities and skills have a far greater chance of landing jobs, promotions, and even higher salaries than those of us who don't. After all, if you don't really believe in yourself, why should anyone else?

So what does it mean to convey confidence on the job—and how do we portray a strong sense of self without coming across as some kind of egotistical blowhard? Here are a few suggestions.

- Confidence isn't arrogance. It's simply a belief in the value of your contribution at work, so don't hesitate to reflect that belief in what you say and do when appropriate. When you hand off an important report to the boss, add: "John, I think you're going to be very pleased with this—the data really shows some improvement in our customer service area." This isn't bragging about you, per se ("Did I mention I graduated with a 4.0?"), but about the value of the work you created. **Warning:** Don't go overboard with this one. Nobody, including your boss, is interested in getting constant reports from you about how great you're doing. After all, good work does speak for itself, and if that's what you're contributing on a regular basis, then your boss will know without you having to point it out.

- Resist the urge to ask for constant feedback or validation from your boss. Sure, feedback is important, and we all want to know that we're on the right track. But asking for too much feedback from the boss makes us appear needy and insecure, not to mention it's time-consuming. It would be great if we knew we were getting an A or a D on the job, but work isn't like that. Trust that you're doing what your boss needs you to be doing—if you aren't, chances are you'll be clued in soon enough.

- If you're feeling shaky in the confidence area, embrace the expression "Fake it till you make it," and act the part, even if you're not 100 percent sure you're the greatest thing since sliced bread. How to get more comfortable showing confidence? Practice! Don't be embarrassed to stand in front of your best friend, husband, girlfriend, or a mirror and practice a few choice phrases you can use on your boss. Try: "John, I've researched the data, spoken with the project managers, and talked to our customers, and the information I've gathered supports what I'm proposing. Can I share what I've uncovered so far?" Practice doing those things that are tough for you, so when you're hit with a tricky question, you'll be able to rise to the occasion like a pro.

- Confidence means you aren't afraid to take initiative, instead of waiting to be told to do something before you make a move. This could mean going the distance to get an answer to a question or investigating possible solutions to a nagging problem (instead of assuming the answer isn't out there or the problem can't be solved) or carving out some extra time on the side to work on other efforts that add value, whether it's researching a new computer supplier for your department or meeting with other employees to learn about their programs or projects. This kind of confidence—where you're thinking about your organization's well-being, and not just your own—is exactly the kind of confidence that your boss loves to see in you.

How else to drive your boss nuts? In addition to the three biggies above, here are a few more no-nos:

Don't surprise your boss, one-up him (especially in public), or do anything else that would prove embarrassing. This includes going over your boss's head and reaching out to your boss's boss. Unless your boss gives you the OK, stay away from his boss. Period. As former fashion executive Valerie Louzonis points out, "Once you go over your boss's head, the trust is violated. And if I can't trust an employee, I won't keep them on my staff."

While we're on the subject of respecting the hierarchy within your organization, make sure you always use the appropriate channels your boss and others have laid out for you, as Lisa Lieberman, administrator at the Evelyn H. Lauder Breast Center at Memorial Sloan-Kettering Cancer Center, points out. "Two junior-level employees had asked to meet with me, but they hadn't met with their own bosses or other supervisors first," says Lieberman, who is responsible for 240 people directly and indirectly in her day-to-day job. "I have an open-door policy, but I sent those employees back to their own supervisors after meeting with them. You always need to work through your own direct channels before you seek advice or help from outside of them," she suggests.

Other boss pet peeves? Laziness, sloppiness, and when employees work too fast to get a job done at the expense of thoroughness or accuracy. And if you disagree with your boss, keep your disagreements between the two of you. Many a career has been sunk by the employee who complained about the boss in an email—only to have the email circulate around the company.

Step #5:
Become a Master of the
Employee-Boss Relationship

Help the Boss Look Good

There was once a slogan from a shampoo commercial that says it all when it comes to the employee-boss relationship: "If you don't look good, we don't look good." If you want a relationship that really rocks, do whatever it takes—as long as it's legal and ethical, of course—to help your boss look good. Be another set of hands, ears, and eyes to help your boss shine, because when you help the boss succeed, chances are that you will, too. How to help your boss look good—even great? It isn't as hard as you might think.

How to Help the Boss Look Good

- Come early, stay late. Not terribly sexy or glamorous, but people notice hard work and respect it.

- Look the part. As we've already covered in previous chapters, appearance counts on the job.

- Act the part. Even if you're the most brilliant multitasker in the world, it doesn't look like you're working when you're emailing a coworker, text-messaging your friend about plans for that night, and listening to an iPod all at once. Be discreet with the gadgets, and keep cell phones for breaks or while you're away from your desk.

- Watch for typos and spelling errors, grammatical mistakes, and anything else that broadcasts "I didn't spend enough time on this" in your emails or other written communication. If your email is going out to your boss, your boss's boss, or others inside the company, it may be worth getting another pair of eyes to proof your message before it goes out, particularly if you're prone to typos.

- Have someone else listen to your voice mail—and make sure it best represents "the team," of you and your boss. As coworkers begin to associate you and your boss together, you can expect plenty of phone calls, emails, and other communications that pertain to you both—so make sure your message is as polished and professional as you are.

- Bring your best to the table. As obvious as it sounds, be prepared as best you can, whether it's for meetings, a brief conference call, or anything that puts you in front of other people. Don't save your best stuff for people "that count"— the truth is that news travels fast, and you want to show that you can always shine, no matter who is asking.

Doing Good Work Helps You and the Boss

The real key to helping your boss look good is doing well yourself. As we've already pointed out, you're the Robin to his Batman, the Skipper to her Barbie. You're the sidekick, the Mini-Me, the boss's representative out there in the office, so delivering good work is really the best thing you can do for him and, therefore, for you.

What does it take to deliver good work? Or excellent work? Ask the boss! Obvious though it may seem, don't overlook this important step. Make sure you really know what your boss expects from you—don't assume you know. For example, Alex Goor, co-president of Instinet, a global agency institutional broker, reports, "I hate drive-by sign-off requests—people who intercept me in the hall on the way to a meeting with an invoice in hand asking for a signature. If it's something important enough to need sign-off, I'm going to need backup information to let me know whether or not it's right to approve and the time to consider that information before approving. This seems obvious, but it's amazing how often it happens. If people would just put themselves in my shoes, they would never come unprepared."

Dos and Don'ts
of Doing Good Work for the Boss

DO *DEMONSTRATE THAT YOU ARE THERE TO DO THE JOB YOU WERE HIRED TO DO*—and whatever else anyone throws your way. Making copies and stapling? Sure, you love it! Your New Professional mantra: "Is there anything else that I can help you with?" Say this often, especially to your boss. As cliché as it sounds, attitude is everything. Nobody likes the newbie who thinks he's got it all figured out or is above doing the grunt work. If you feel temporarily bored, suck it up, smile, and remind yourself that great things are ahead—because they are, as long as you're able and willing to play the cards you've been dealt now.

DO *UNDERSTAND WHAT A DAY IN YOUR BOSS'S LIFE IS LIKE.* What is her agenda? What kind of results is she responsible for? What are her objectives, goals, problems to solve—and how can you help?

DO *LISTEN TO YOUR BOSS.* When she's explaining something to you, don't interrupt, don't half-listen while you're rehearsing a brilliant response in your mind—just listen. Force yourself to pause, breathe, and think before you respond or react.

DON'T *FORGET TO KEEP A WRITTEN FILE OF YOUR ACCOMPLISHMENTS, EFFORTS, AND OTHER ACHIEVEMENTS ON THE JOB.* One suggestion: Email yourself a "Top 10 Accomplishments" list every week, and keep the lists on file. Once every three months, send your boss a written update of what you've been working on. Don't assume your boss knows all the brilliant work you've been doing. Make sure he knows before your performance review rolls around, and you'll be one step (in fact, many steps) ahead of the game.

DON'T *TRY TO BE THE ROCK STAR OR PRESIDENT JUST YET.* It's tempting to want to come into a new job, make a splash, and try to contribute in a big way. To repeat: Your boss has a job he or she needs you to get done. Do that job. Save the big contribution for United Way for the time being.

Getting Feedback from the Boss

One final thought when it comes to doing good work on the job: Don't wait for your annual review to receive feedback from your boss. Make sure you know you're on track by asking questions: "Is there anything else you'd like me to keep in mind when I do this assignment next month?" "Is there any other feedback you'd like to share?" Proceed with

caution here, as there is a fine line between soliciting feedback and seeming overly needy.

Whether the feedback is about your work on a project,
the outfit you wore last week, or anything else, handle it like
a pro. Receive the criticism with open arms, and keep the
following tips in mind:

- As hard as it is, resist the urge to be defensive, argue on
  your own behalf, or do anything else along these lines.
  Even if you're as right as rain, any attempt to explain
  yourself will appear immature and unprofessional—not
  the look we are going for.

- Be thankful for the feedback, even if it hurts. After all,
  when you know what you're doing wrong, you can fix it.
  Because of your boss's criticism, you're just one step
  closer to sheer perfection.

- When you receive feedback, let your boss know you're trying to change. For instance: "John, thanks for making me
  aware of my communication style and how it may be rubbing people the wrong way. I want to let you know that I'm
  working with a coach to improve my speaking skills."

- A few weeks after you receive feedback, be proactive and
  check back in with the boss to make sure the issue is re-
  solved. Make sure the problem really is fixed, so that it
  doesn't come back to haunt you in a future performance
  review.

In the Final Analysis

If there's one thing to remember when it comes to your boss, it's that it's up to you to make the most of your situation, even if your boss is less than great. No matter how lousy your boss is (and I sincerely hope this isn't the case), it isn't an excuse for being lousy on the job. Instead, remember that bosses come and go throughout a career, and this is simply a small bump in the road. When the boss chips are down, resolve to focus more than ever on results and deliverables, and do the good work you were hired to do. And if it doesn't work out perfectly—or at all—don't worry too much. You've probably learned a few things along the way (even if it's what not to do as a boss!) and you're better armed, better prepared, and better able to handle the next boss who comes along.

SECTION III

You at Work

UNSPOKEN RULE #7

Climb the Corporate Ladder with Subtle—but Shameless— Self-Promotion

Learn Why It Takes More than Doing Great Work to Get Promoted on the Job

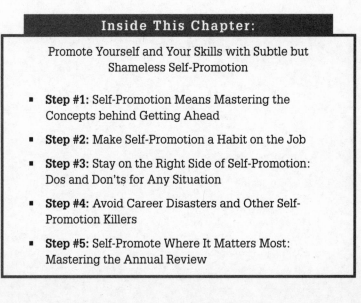

Inside This Chapter:

Promote Yourself and Your Skills with Subtle but Shameless Self-Promotion

- **Step #1:** Self-Promotion Means Mastering the Concepts behind Getting Ahead

- **Step #2:** Make Self-Promotion a Habit on the Job

- **Step #3:** Stay on the Right Side of Self-Promotion: Dos and Don'ts for Any Situation

- **Step #4:** Avoid Career Disasters and Other Self-Promotion Killers

- **Step #5:** Self-Promote Where It Matters Most: Mastering the Annual Review

Introduction:
Why Bother with Self-Promotion?

Once we enter the workplace, most of us assume that the employees who work the hardest, are the smartest, or produce the best results are the same ones who wind up with the best projects, the most interesting opportunities—even the bigger raises and better promotions. After all, this kind of work-reward pattern makes sense; in school, the students who studied the most and worked the hardest usually got the As—right?

Right . . . sometimes. And sometimes the A students were the ones who didn't spend too much time hitting the books, but who seemed to have a knack for acing the tests. Perhaps you remember A students who weren't the smartest ones at all; instead, they were the ones who participated frequently in class or asked the most questions to earn their high marks. Even more annoying, you may have known one or two A students who could barely add, but were loved and adored by all—especially the teachers.

For all you valedictorians reading, rest assured that most students with good grades earned them and deserved them, fair and square. But we also know that justice doesn't always prevail in quite the same way on the job. This isn't to suggest that hard work, producing results, and intelligence aren't key factors for success at work; in fact, it's hard to imagine any real progress on the job without these qualities. Still,

208 ELIZABETH FREEDMAN, M.B.A.

consider the fact that the best folks on the job aren't necessarily the ones with the best titles or salaries, just like the
best actors don't always win the Oscar at the Academy
Awards each year.

Ultimately, success at work isn't as simple as doing a
great job and getting the equivalent of an A from your
boss—after all, what if you have the kind of boss who travels frequently and is hardly around to see the great work you
are doing in the first place? The truth is that with a busy
workforce, employees who travel and work remotely, and
plenty of other distractions on your coworkers' minds, you
can't assume that *anyone* is necessarily seeing and remem-
bering the great work you do. You can't assume that
others—like your manager—know about the great feedback
you just got from a client, for instance, unless you make it
known in some way. And that's where we come in.

Step #1:
Self-Promotion Means Mastering the Concepts behind Getting Ahead

So, what does it take to really succeed on the job and in our
careers? How do we make sure that the powers that be
know how we're actually contributing without making a nui-
sance of ourselves? Most important, how can we employ
simple, sincere tactics of self-promotion, minus the arrogance or attitude, to really get noticed in the workplace? Start
by understanding a few key success principles and concepts
for getting ahead on the job.

It's the Savvy Wheel—Not the Squeaky One— that Gets the Grease

Many of us have heard the old adage that "the squeaky wheel gets the grease." In workplace terms, this suggests that those who speak up, and often, are more likely to land the promotion, the better opportunities, or the raise over those who stay silent. As a result, some of us have no problem with letting others know what we're contributing. After all, we've got to advertise in order for people to know what we're selling, right?

Consider the perspective of Kevin Giglinto, vice president of sales and marketing for the Chicago Symphony Orchestra: "Employees who communicate most clearly are best positioned for recognition, but it's not really about being a squeaky wheel. It's timing your communication and delivering it in a professional and concise way. In the end, if you deliver, and can communicate results, you'll be fine. I have never seen a 'squeaky wheel' get recognized in front of others who have delivered more and were more professional."

In other words, there is a clear distinction between self-promotion and sounding obnoxious and arrogant, so be sure to keep yourself in check here. Tooting your own horn is a smart, savvy move when done right; blaring a siren about your work in the ears of your managers and coworkers will only drive everyone else nuts.

When It Comes to Success, Beauty Is in the Eye of the Beholder

What does it take to succeed at work? Depending on where you work, and for whom you work, that answer varies considerably, so start by understanding how success is defined in workplace terms, which may differ somewhat from your own. For example, if your manager defines success by how many hours you put in at your desk, you know that arriving early and leaving late will score you some points. On the other hand, your boss might care far more about the kind of results you're generating than when you come and go, so the fact that you've hit your quota or target may be the only thing on her mind. In other words, once you know what your supervisor values, you'll know what to draw attention to and emphasize to your supervisor when appropriate.

Only Success Can Promote a Good Product

Real career success isn't about trying to master the world of office politics, being the world's best schmoozer, or otherwise using a lot of slick moves, gloss, or snake oil to mask a so-so performance on the job. You can be the world's best salesperson, but if the product is shoddy, your sales pitch will only carry you so far. If you're not doing the best job you can do, no amount of self-promotion will help you. Don't spend so much time maneuvering for the next promotion or worrying about the raise you think you should be getting that you forget what it takes to land these goodies in the first place.

Success at Work Means
Showing Your Enthusiasm for the Job

When do people work hardest in their careers? For some of us, it happens during the job search itself—after all, we all want to land opportunities that make us excited to get out of bed in the morning. Most of us keep our noses to the grindstone when we start that job, working hard to impress, learn the ropes, and figure out our roles and responsibilities. But after a few months at work, some of us start to take that hard-won job for granted. We get lax with our wardrobe choices, or come in a bit later than we used to. Worse, we start to put less effort into our work, become bored, or just don't care like we did early on. Sure, we all have days where the job is less than a thrill a minute, but if this feels like you on a regular basis, watch out. Success on the job and in your career means keeping the enthusiasm, excitement, and drive alive for the work you do, and making sure that the powers that be know that you're appreciative for the job you have and that you're happy to be there.

Success Is an Ongoing Process of Improvement and Reinvention

For a moment, think of your career like a product on a supermarket shelf. Like any good product, you've got certain ingredients—or characteristics of success—that make us want to buy. Your job as a product? Keep us wanting to buy again, and again, and again. This may mean adding new ingredients to the mix—for example, you could master a new foreign language or computer program. Or you may come up with your own version of "new and improved!" where you're developing new skills, taking on bigger responsibilities, and learning new things, keeping your "buyers" as excited about you now as they were when they first met you.

Step #2:
Make Self-Promotion a Habit on the Job

It's one thing to read about these success principles on paper, but it's entirely another to integrate these ideas into your life and make them habits on the job. After all, self-promotion really boils down to selling yourself in a way that's professional, subtle, and polished, and sales is no walk in the park. Even if you hate the thought of sales, or haven't ever sold a thing in your life, just check out the number of laundry detergents on your average supermarket shelf. Between the lemon-fresh scent, the color-safe bleach, and the new-and-improved formula, these poor guys are fighting for your attention, day after day.

Since there are so many detergents out there, companies that sell them develop deliberate strategies to grab your attention and entice you to buy their product. And while you may be a sucker for a cute red bottle or for a lemon-fresh scent, truly successful companies know that the only way to your wallet is by demonstrating to you, over and over, that their product is somehow different and better than the others. The same applies to you on the job. Get comfortable with selling and promoting your skills in a way that delivers, and you'll be reaping the benefits, too. How to begin? Read on below.

Advertise

This tip involves one simple concept: visibility! For people to know more about who you are and the value you bring to the table, they've got to know you exist and be reminded of this fact. In order to raise your profile, consider joining a committee at work (how about organizing a group to support a local charity or run the spring softball team?) or writing the office newsletter. Volunteer at the next big event or invite your coworkers out to lunch. Create opportunities to (1) meet new people within the office and (2) demonstrate your skills and competency on the job. Give people the chance to see you in action and they'll remember you long after the softball team wins the big game.

Let Other People Sing Your Praises

When exceptional things are said about you, don't keep it to yourself. If a customer raves about how he's so pleased with the job you did for him, ask him if he'd be kind enough to put his feedback in a short email to your boss. Don't be shy or hesitate to take this step. You've only asked him to repeat what he said, and this feedback makes a big difference, so ask! Remember, this is helpful information to your organization, too; you'd probably be hard-pressed to find someone in your marketing or PR departments who wouldn't love to have a great customer testimonial in writing, so when you ask for this information, you're helping out your company, not just yourself.

Measure Your Progress with Facts and Figures

No matter where you work or what you do, chances are that your manager will be moved by numbers, facts, and figures. Hard, cold data is always compelling because it's objective: It's easier to argue with an opinion or disagree with a point of view than with data that's grounded in research. Take advantage of this by keeping track of what you do and the results you bring, and put this data into reports, spreadsheets, graphs, or some other quantifiable format that really measures what you do on an ongoing basis. If you work in something that's dollar-driven, for instance, this task should be pretty easy. For example: "Increased sales by 22 percent from last quarter, contributing to a 38 percent increase in revenue for our new product line." Think about how you can quantify what you do: Did you train more new employees? Write two new newsletters? Improve patient waiting time at the hospital? Gather metrics and share this information with your boss—she'll concretely see the value you contribute to the big picture and see how you're improving over time.

Keep Track of Your Career Progress with a Summary of Accomplishments

Not only should you send your boss positive feedback and data on occasion, but you should also keep a general report or summary of all of your accomplishments. (**Helpful hint:** Keep a running report on an ongoing basis—if you wait until the last minute to pull this together, you'll inevitably forget your accomplishments from months ago and leave things out.)

What goes in this Summary of Accomplishments? It might contain samples of your work, letters or emails of positive feedback you've received, more data that quantifies your results, lists of your achievements, summaries of activities or projects you've worked on, and more. Then, a week or so before your annual review (or other formal meetings where things like promotions and salary are discussed), send your manager the report you've compiled—or simply offer the report on a quarterly basis to keep him informed and updated. Give him a chance to review what you've done over the year so that he'll be in the right frame of mind when you sit down to discuss your career. Once again, it pays to know your organization's culture when trying out this strategy. While many managers might appreciate having a summary of your work, others may feel like you've gone overboard. The message? Before you try this on for size, be sure it will be received in the spirit in which it was intended.

Conduct Research

Want to make sure you're on the right track when it comes to self-promotion and the work you do? Ask a few trusted coworkers about your work style. If they had to change one thing about you at work, what would it be and why? Keep in mind that most people aren't comfortable delivering feedback directly, so you'll have to rely on subtler clues to get your data. For example, you might ask: "Jane, you saw me deliver my last presentation. Is there anything you think I should change for the next one?" or "Alan, can I get your honest opinion about the last few reports I've sent out?" Ask questions about what you've done—instead of about you, directly—and you'll probably capture important feedback about both in doing so.

Go Where No Employee Has Gone Before

If you work in an environment that's filled with plenty of shameless self-promoters, type A personalities, and rock stars, you know that you're probably not the only one who'd like to be considered for great projects or juicy opportunities. Break away from the pack by charting your own course—within reason. Take the initiative to work on something new, something that solves a problem, or something that others haven't touched, either because they haven't thought of it, or simply because the project is a pain in the butt that no one else has the patience to deal with. As long as your new initiative is OK with the boss and doesn't interfere with your current responsibilities and, most important, adds value to your department or organization, why not take it on? Or, "Focus on becoming an expert in a new area," suggests Lisa Wilson, a health insurance specialist with the United States Department of Health & Human Services. Working within the organization's Centers for Medicare & Medicaid Services, Lisa realized that she was one of the younger employees on the job, and found herself surrounded by talented professionals who had plenty of experience to offer. Suddenly Lisa's entire organization was at the center of the biggest modernization to hit Medicare in 40 years, and she decided to learn as much as she could about the changes impacting millions of Americans. "Even though I haven't had as much time under my belt as some of my coworkers, I know as much as they do when it comes to these changes. I'm now regarded by my coworkers as having a strong expertise in this area, despite my age or overall work experience."

Here's another example: When I worked at a large nonprofit organization as a fund-raiser in my second job after college, I realized that we weren't approaching a large portion of the legal community for support. With my boss's permission, I organized the nonprofit's first-ever fund-raising event to target this population, which I did on the side in addition to my regular fund-raising responsibilities. The result? We raised additional dollars for our organization's cause, and I was also given the opportunity to manage a small team for this event, which was experience I needed and hadn't obtained until that point. Best of all? I was recognized by our senior vice president at an all-staff meeting for the results, got plenty of nice emails from coworkers for my efforts, and even received a very congratulatory handwritten note from our organization's president. Worth the effort? I'd do it again in a heartbeat.

Ignore Self-Promotion at Your Own Risk

If you shy away from promoting yourself on the job because you think it's bragging, it's arrogant, or it makes you look like a conceited oaf, think again. Others think any kind of self-promotion is good old-fashioned BS and totally unnecessary, and that good work should speak for itself. Finally, self-promotion is often ignored by those of us who are shy and just not used to talking about ourselves.

It's tempting to ignore the habit of self-promotion, for whatever reason; it isn't easy, and it takes extra time and requires risk, no doubt about it. In an ideal world, where your manager is a terrific leader who is always going to bat for you and making your accomplishments known, you wouldn't have to worry too much about stuff like raises or getting promotions. But don't count on it.

This isn't because you don't have a great boss, but no boss, no matter how terrific, knows you as well as you do. Only *you* really know what you've been doing, what you've accomplished, and you've got to be willing to be an advocate for yourself. Don't leave this job to anyone else or think that anyone else will do it for you.

If you hate the thought of doing this, consider how you can take small steps to help your career through some of the suggestions offered. Remind yourself that other people out there, every day, in your workplace, are promoting themselves in ways that produce results for them, so don't get left on the sidelines. Instead, choose the outcomes that you really want—whether it's a new position, a new location, or simply more responsibilities on the job—and consider the self-promotion tactics that can help you get them.

Step #3:
Stay on the Right Side of Self-Promotion: Dos and Don'ts for Any Situation

As I stated earlier, trying to sell a product that isn't working just doesn't work, no matter how great your self-promotional skills may be. But when it comes to the workplace, it isn't enough to simply avoid being a bad or so-so "product"— your job is to be the kind of product that people can't get enough of, that they rave about to their coworkers, that they use over and over again. In short, you want to be indispensable. Keep in mind, being the kind of employee that others rave about doesn't mean that we're working around the clock or killing ourselves to be appreciated.

Be the Best Product You Can Be: Dos and Don'ts for Self-Promotion

DO *IMITATE.* The fact is that in any office, competition exists. I don't mean this in a cutthroat kind of way, but recognize that plenty of talent is already out there. If you want what some of your more successful coworkers have, do what they do. Better yet, ask people who have what you want out for coffee or lunch. Prepare plenty of questions, listen, and find out what works for them when it comes to success on the job. (By the way, if someone is gracious enough to give you their time, don't argue or contradict their advice. Take it for what it's worth, and leave out the stuff like "That would never work for me, because . . ." After all, if they are more successful than you, they've got something to say.)

DO *COMMIT TO YOUR JOB.* Dedicate yourself to knowing more about your industry and profession, and gaining expertise in your particular area. Join your profession's national association and local chapter, and go to their meetings and conferences. Attend seminars and lectures, and be willing to take vacation days and pay for this kind of stuff yourself if your company won't ante up, because the type of learning you'll get—and, more important, the people you'll meet— will be worth its weight in gold.

DO *BE AMBITIOUS.* "It's amazing what a difference a little initiative can make," says Alex Goor, co-president of Instinet, a global agency institutional broker. "I am sure I got promoted because of one incident early in my career. Our president asked a large group of people in the company to do a little, simple extra-credit homework. I ended up being the only person to do it. When the president starting asking the group questions, I was the only one able to answer them and offer ideas. As a result, I came to the president's attention in a favorable light and started getting more and more responsibility directly from him that ultimately led me to where I am now. Just taking the initiative to do something anyone could have done put me on the path to success."

DO *MAKE AN EFFORT TO GET ALONG WITH PEOPLE AT ALL DIFFERENT AGES AND LEVELS.* When people are new to the workforce, they're often surprised at how they are frequently the youngest person in the office. For some, this isn't a big deal—after all, once you start working together, you'll focus more on what you have in common and less on your differences. On the other hand, many of us tend to spend time around people our own age and aren't used to being around people who are our parents' or grandparents' age (unless they actually *are* our parents or grandparents) on a regular basis, so we're not quite as comfortable conversing, making chitchat, and generally building relationships with people of different ages. Just remember: Your coworkers aren't your parents, no matter what their age, so act as professionally with them as you would anyone else.

DON'T *FORGET WHERE YOU SIT ON THE TOTEM POLE.* Every office has a pecking order and hierarchy, so pay homage to yours, too. There's a fine line between taking initiative and sidestepping protocol, and success at work means recognizing the chain of command, even if it seems inefficient and antiquated to you. If it drives you nuts to get ten different people to approve every memo you write, talk to your boss and see if you can cut out a layer or two in the bureaucracy. Still, don't hold your breath on this one. The reality is that most people have more knowledge about how things work than you, so your goal, at least in the beginning, is to work as best you can within the system—not to change or ignore the system.

DON'T *ASSUME THAT OPPORTUNITY ISN'T ALWAYS KNOCKING.* In other words, use any chance you get as a moment to demonstrate your talents. Don't put the minimal effort into something because "nobody will read it anyway," or show up looking sloppy because you sit in your cubicle all day. Trust me, the one piece of work you decide to blow off will be the one assignment your boss decides to take a close look at. As far as you're concerned, every day is game day, so keep your guard up and be ready for opportunities to shine.

DON'T *GET TOO HUNG UP ON HOW THINGS "SHOULD BE" AT WORK.* Sure, work is filled with annoyances, like bureaucracy, office politics, hypocrisy, and plenty more, but keep your attitude in check. True, this is easier said than done, but everybody gets driven nuts by work sometimes; when you voice your complaints, you'll be seen as a complainer, or unable to handle change, or as someone who doesn't have the history or perspective on the job to understand why things are the way they are. At the very least, you'll look like someone who has expectations that are out of whack; so even if you are as right as rain, keep your thoughts to yourself and let it go. As Lisa Wilson, a 28-year-old government employee, points out, "It's easy to be flip about changes or the new management flavor of the month, but you're going to have to do it anyway, so why not make the most of it and try to learn something?"

DON'T *STAY HIDDEN IN YOUR CUBICLE ALL DAY.* Don't keep your nose so close to the grindstone that your coworkers have no idea who you are and what you do. Make the effort to get out—eat lunch with other people, get involved by serving on a project or committee outside of your job description; do anything to connect with others. Get invited to meetings (as discussed in Chapter Three) or go to programs and events that are related to your profession.

Give Me a Slice of That Humble Pie: Whatever You Sell, Make Sure Humility Is Part of It

"Your first job is about your second job."

When you start a job after graduating from college or at an early stage in your career, recognize what you bring to the table. Unless you've graduated having discovered the secret to world peace or the cure for cancer, or invented a new gizmo that the rest of us can't live without, most of us don't enter the working world with much expertise or work experience, not to mention a real understanding of a particular business, industry, competitors, customers, etc. The reality is that it just takes a while to learn the ropes and add some real value to wherever it is you work, no matter how smart you are.

That's why it's so irritating to others when New Professionals try to negotiate unrealistically high starting salaries, have out-of-whack expectations about how fast they will be climbing up the company ladder, or have an attitude of "you're lucky to have me," according to David Roberts, president and CEO of Equity Methods, a stock valuation company based in Phoenix, Arizona. In other words, don't try to sell or promote something where you don't have credibility—stick to emphasizing those qualities that you're already recognized for, like hard work and a positive attitude. "If you show up with a 'me first' attitude, you'll shoot yourself in the foot, fast. It will come up in performance reviews, it will impact opportunities for leadership, and, ultimately, that attitude will hurt your career."

What works best? According to Roberts, "Have a good attitude, work hard, and let people know that 'I'm here to contribute.' When we have people like that, we don't want to let them go. We'll promote them and give them raises often—because humility and character are so important to us."

Ultimately, suggests Roberts, remember what your first job is all about—contributing, working hard, and learning as much as you can so that you're successfully positioned for a terrific second job.

Step #4:
Avoid Career Disasters and Other Self-Promotion Killers

"Dear Liz"

Self-Promotion Disasters: When a Good Thing Goes Bad

As we've stated earlier, when it comes to selling yourself and your skills on the job, tread carefully—very carefully. Confused yet? We've been saying that you've got to be your own advocate without being arrogant, and we advise you to take initiative, but not so much that you scare everyone off. The fact is that when it comes to self-promotion, a little goes a long way, so tone down your efforts if you think you're going overboard. But if you're still unsure how to handle life as an unabashed self-promoter on the job, ask Liz!

Dear Liz:
    I don't think I need to self-promote. The fact is that my boss tells me that I'm doing a great job, and I've been promoted twice in the 18 months I've been here. Do I really need to bother with this stuff?
    Sincerely,
    Already a Rock Star

Dear Rock Star:

Even Clinton had to campaign for reelection. It's great that you're doing a fantastic job, but don't rest on your laurels. Things change on the job all the time—your boss could leave, your organization could restructure, and your job could change as a result—so you'll want to be in the best position possible to handle anything that comes up. You may not need to employ all the strategies discussed, but at the very least, keep an ongoing record of your accomplishments, and collect all that good feedback about you in writing—you never know when you'll need it.

Dear Liz:

In theory, I have no problem with self-promotion—I believe in myself and what I contribute. But in practice, I can't seem to bring myself to do it. It all seems so cheesy and forced, and I hate the idea of forwarding emails so my boss knows what a great job I'm doing. Isn't it her job to know this already?

Sincerely,

Skeptical of Self-Promotion

Dear Skeptic:

Let me ask you a question: How is your system working for you? If your career is moving at the pace and in the direction that you'd like, then let us speak no more of this self-promotion. On the other hand, it's tempting to think that our boss will simply notice what we do, or that the good work we do will speak for itself. But does anyone at work—besides your boss—really know what it is that you do? Don't get caught in the trap of thinking that just because you do a great job this will be recognized by everyone, and be careful about refusing to "play games"—self-promotion and selling yourself are what successful people do every day. Managing your career and taking proactive steps to ensure that you're moving ahead isn't "cheesy"—it may just be something you're not used to doing, so start small and ease yourself into it.

Dear Liz:

I graduated from college two years ago and have been working at a small nonprofit ever since. Since then, my job responsibilities and duties have not changed, even though I've hinted around that I'm more than ready for more challenges on the job. Is there anything I can do in terms of self-promotion to get more job responsibilities? I feel like I'm never going to advance here.

Sincerely,

Data Entry Slave

Dear Data Entry Slave:

Embarking on a one-man (or one-woman) self-promotion campaign isn't recommended here. After all, your organization is small, and it's likely that your work and contributions are already getting noticed by the powers that be, so this isn't an issue of visibility or needing to toot your own horn.

The question is, how are your contributions regarded? To be blunt, even though you think you're "more than ready" for more challenges, does everyone else agree? Keep in mind that many new employees stay in positions for longer than two years (in fact, three is average), so be sure that your expectations are reasonable. However, if everyone around you is getting promoted *except* you, then it may be time to sit down and talk with your supervisor (don't just "hint") about what you need to do in order to be considered for more opportunities down the road.

Finally, don't wait to be handed more responsibilities on the job. In fact, your boss might be waiting for *you* to take this initiative. "I want to see that you are capable of already doing work at the next level before I promote you to the next level," shared former fashion executive Valerie Louzonis. She adds, "Offer to assist when the need arises and offer to stay late to get a project done. Professionals are not clock-watchers." The moral of the story? Take the step to work on other projects with the boss's approval (without neglecting your day-to-day work) so that you can show others you're ready to take on bigger challenges when the time comes.

Career Disasters: When No Amount of Self-Promotion Can Save You

You've worked hard to land your job and impress the folks at work, and you're doing your best to keep things running smoothly. Sure, we all hit a bump in the road every now and then, but there are a few major potholes you'll want to avoid in your career, or you'll end up with a lot more grief than a flat tire.

Career Disaster #1:
"If I don't get promoted soon, I'm out of here!"

Well, friend, best start packing your bags. As we shared earlier, nothing turns folks off more than a sense of entitlement on the job, so watch yourself here and lose the unrealistic expectations. If you really do feel this way, keep this stuff to yourself: One new employee at a large consulting firm mentioned to a couple of coworkers at lunch one day that she thought she should have been hired at a more senior level. The next thing you know, that employee's boss—and *his boss*—had heard about her comments and were none too pleased. The fact is that when you signed on the dotted line, you agreed to do the job you have now. If you feel you were promised a five-course meal and were given McDonald's instead, that's a different story; otherwise, hang on with the knowledge that if you do a good job, you probably won't be in this role much longer, anyway.

Career Disaster #2: "My job is incredibly boring!"

Let's face it: Most entry-level jobs require some grunt work that isn't necessarily as challenging as the kinds of things we've done before. But rest assured, you won't be stuck in your role forever. After all, your company has invested time and money in you, and they want you to stick around, learn the ropes, and get promoted—when *they* think you're ready. In the meantime, love the job you're with.

Career Disaster #3: "This job sucks! I'm out of here!"

According to a 2004 Harris Interactive Poll, many employees in the United States dislike their jobs, feel burned out, and generally have a negative attitude about their employers and senior managers—and these numbers are higher among employees ages 18 to 34. For instance, only 37 percent of younger workers report that a good deal of pride comes from work, and 47 percent of younger employees report feeling burned out on the job (The Harris Poll, June 2–16, 2004).

Unfortunately, there are dozens of reasons why someone might be dissatisfied with a job—and, sometimes, this has nothing to do with the job or company itself. For example, do you frequently say yes when you want to say no? Have you been willing to communicate with your boss and others about what you need? If you've had a few bad days or weeks, it's easy to get caught in a negative spiral at work, or to hang around with other negative people who focus on everything that is wrong instead of right. Sometimes our own personality quirks get in the way: For instance, if you're the kind of person who takes things very personally, work isn't going to be easy, no matter where you go, because feedback and constructive criticism happen anywhere.

Sure, sometimes you aren't in the right job or the right place, and it is time to leave. However, for many of us, getting used to life at work *is* work and takes time, and the grass is not necessarily greener someplace else. Don't be so quick to run out the door when the going gets tough; as we'll discuss in a later chapter, hopping from job to job never looks good on a résumé, and you have everything to gain by sticking things out for a reasonable period of time and trying to improve your situation—not to mention, plenty to lose if you quit abruptly.

Step #5:
Self-Promote Where It Matters Most: Mastering the Annual Review

If there was ever a time to self-promote like you never have before, your performance review would be it. Typically conducted annually or semiannually, the review is that time of year when you and the boss sit down for a heart-to-heart. More specifically, it's the formal meeting—often mandatory throughout the company—that can decide plenty about you and your career, including bonus amounts, promotions, and salary increases for the upcoming year. It's a time to get feedback, ask questions, and make your thoughts, concerns, and hopes for the future known. In short, it's the meeting of all meetings as far as your career is concerned, so you'll want to do everything you can to make sure your review shines.

Self-Promotion for Superstars: When You Want to Pull out All the Stops

Want to rock the review? It's nothing you can't handle. Check out our tips below so that your review is the slam dunk you want it to be.

- *TIP #1:* When it comes to your review, preparation is key. Don't walk in and try to wing it; do your homework ahead of time. This includes compiling a list of questions to ask and making sure you have your talking points ready. Be prepared, so that when you walk out of that meeting, you don't think of 20 things you wish you had said.

- *TIP #2:* Have your Summary of Accomplishments ready for your review. As we stated earlier, compile this report and present it to the boss a week or two before the big day. Refer to the report during the meeting—this gives you some nice, solid documentation to support your contributions during the year. Keep in mind that this strategy isn't appropriate for every industry or workplace; know your office culture and practices so that you don't overdo it here. And remember, your review isn't show-and-tell— it's a chance to genuinely learn about what's working and what isn't for the future, so don't let your past accomplishments get in the way of talking about what's next for you.

- *TIP #3:* Accept your boss's feedback and suggestions for improvement in a diplomatic, positive way without getting defensive. If you're unsure—or even disagree—with a comment, ask questions in a nonthreatening way: *"John, can you give me an example of when that came up? How might I have handled it better?"*

- *TIP #4:* Now is the time to state your case. If you think it's time for a promotion, or you'd like to be considered for one in the next six months, speak up. Whatever it is you're going for, don't state your wishes without explaining how this will help the company. **Repeat:** Whatever it is you want, explain it in terms that demonstrate your desire to contribute to the organization at a higher level. Don't let your desire for a promotion or more responsibility give the impression that you only care about you and your career, as opposed to caring about your team and your organization.

- *TIP #5:* Stating Your Case, Part II—When you make your wishes known to the boss, offer plenty of supporting evidence, data, documentation, and other "proof" that you're ready. For example, if you'd like to sit in on more meetings with bigwigs, say: *"Mary, I'd like to be considered for more project work, and here's why: In the past six months, I've supported our department on four different projects, I've gotten terrific feedback in writing from one of our largest partners. . . ."* Make sure that whatever you ask for, you're standing on very solid ground, so stick to asking for those things where you've got a solid track record and documented history of success.

- *TIP #6:* Come up with a strategy for handling objections. Remember, this is a sales meeting, and your customer may have reasons why he doesn't want to buy. Be ready for these by anticipating where your boss might disagree with you so that you're ready to respond. This doesn't mean that you argue with the boss or downplay his concerns; instead, acknowledge his point of view, and respectfully offer information or evidence that supports your claims. If he still isn't going for it, drop it, and move on to an area where you both can agree.

- *TIP #7:* Prioritize your wish list. You might have a wish list that is a foot long, but keep your expectations realistic: You may not walk out of that review with promises of big raises or promotions. Instead, pick one or two things that you'd really like to have on the job, and make those the priority for discussion.

- *TIP #8:* Don't overwhelm the boss with information. While it's fine to reference your Summary of Accomplishments and have your talking points ready, don't overdo it. Think about three to five main ideas or points that you want to get across, and emphasize those throughout the meeting in different ways. To help you narrow your focus, think about your review this way: If your meeting was only ten minutes long, what would be the three most important things you'd want your boss to know about your performance before he left the room?

- *TIP #9:* As much as some of us would love to steer the entire conversation and outcome of our review, this meeting is a two-way street, and your boss is running the show. Do plenty of listening, don't interrupt, and, once again, don't argue or get defensive with his comments. No matter how much you disagree, you'll only come off looking like a jerk if you contradict him.

- *TIP #10:* A review isn't time for surprises. By the time you're ready for your review, you should have a pretty good sense of how this meeting is going to go, and that's because you and your manager should have a constant flow of communication throughout the year. Hopefully, your manager is playing a proactive role in ensuring this is happening. But if your manager isn't the talking type, make sure you are still receiving information and feedback on a regular basis. (See our chapter on working with your boss for more tips here.)

- *TIP #11:* Don't feel obligated to wait until the clock strikes 12 to make known your desires for a promotion, increased responsibility, or a raise. This doesn't mean that you hound your boss around the clock, but waiting once a year for your annual review to roll around may be longer than necessary. Keep in mind that some companies are very by-the-book, where increases in salary or title can only happen at certain times of the year, but if this isn't the case, strike while the iron is hot. If you've just done a bang-up job on a project, have won an award, or been recognized for your good work in some way, ask for what you want now, while your success is still fresh in the boss's mind. You may still have to wait awhile before your title or salary gets bumped up, but at least you've planted the seed and set the stage for an even more productive annual review.

- *TIP #12:* Practice before the big day. It's not easy for some of us to ask for what we want—particularly when it comes to money. Rehearse before your review: Stand in front of a mirror and get comfortable stating your case in a positive, enthusiastic way, so that you've got your script ready when your review rolls around. Your review is a conversation about you, so the more comfortable you are talking about your work, the better.

- *TIP #13:* Remember, an annual review—or any meeting with your manager, for that matter—may not go like clockwork. Think of this discussion as a negotiation, so always have Plan B in your back pocket. For instance, if your boss can't offer you a raise because there is an organization-wide salary freeze, what else could you ask for? If you are told you aren't ready for a promotion, find out if you can revisit the issue with your boss in six months. And don't forget—part of your job is to leave that meeting feeling like you've both won. Say things like, *"What would work best for you?" "How can I make your job easier this year?" "Can you offer me some suggestions for how I can contribute at a higher level?"* All go a very long way in showing that you care about both of you.

Show Me the Money!
Talking about Salary in a
Performance Review

Be ready to discuss salary during your annual review by having plenty of information to support your desire for a raise, bigger bonus, or whatever other aspects of compensation (increased vacation days, more flextime, working from home, etc.) you're going for. If you think you're entitled to a raise, explain why. Be specific: What did you accomplish, and what was the value of your accomplishments to your department and organization? In other words, did your work allow the company to save time, make more money, acquire new customers, hire better people, deliver an improved level of customer service? What was the

234 ELIZABETH FREEDMAN, M.B.A.

real impact that you had over the course of the year in dollar terms?

As part of your preparation to discuss compensation, be sure to benchmark what other people are making, too, so that you don't ask for something that is unrealistically high or lower than what you could be earning. This doesn't mean you ask your peers at work about their salaries—in fact, compensation should only be discussed with your manager, period. But you can find out what other professionals at your level, and in your geographic region of the country, are earning on average. Go online and do salary research at any of the dozens of Web sites out there that allow you to see salary ranges for just about any profession. By the way, use this same tip when preparing to discuss salary at a new job—this information comes in very handy when negotiating salary during a job interview, too.

Looking for some helpful Web sites for salary info? Here are a few:

Jobstar.org—an extremely comprehensive Web site that lists a wide array of salary information for many different professions.

http://jobstar.org/tools/salary/sal-prof.php

Salary.com—another comprehensive Web site with plenty of information about pay levels and other compensation-related information.

http://www.salary.com/home/layoutscripts/homl_display.asp

Monster.com—a user-friendly salary wizard is available here, under Monster's Salary Center. Enter your job title and zip code to get a free "basic" report for general salary information.

http://salary.monster.com/

U.S. Department of Labor, Bureau of Labor Statistics home-page—provides comprehensive information about wages, earnings, and benefits by occupation, geographic region, and much more.

http://stats.bls.gov/

Self-promotion isn't for the faint of heart, and it doesn't come naturally to all of us. That's why the more you are willing to implement these tips, strategies, and suggestions, the easier it will get. Like any habit you're developing, you might stumble in the beginning, feel uncomfortable when making your accomplishments known, or simply be intimidated to bring up issues of your career path or salary with your manager. But take the risk—you don't do you or your career any favors by playing it safe and staying quiet. Find the balance that works best for you between self-promotion and keeping your nose to the grindstone, and you'll see your efforts pay off in ways you couldn't imagine.

UNSPOKEN RULE #8

Burning Bridges Is for Arsonists

Leave Your Job with Class—and Take Intelligent Risks to Land Your Next Job

READY TO JUMP SHIP? Sick of your job and want a new one? Time for graduate school or a trip abroad? You're not the only one who feels that way. Between 50 and 80 percent of all college graduates leave their first job within three years of landing it, according to Holton's *The New Professional,* and studies show that people change several careers in a lifetime. What does this mean to you? Plenty of job-searching and everything that goes along with it, including networking, résumé writing, interviewing, and more.

Like everything else we've discussed so far, there is a right way—and a wrong way—to handle these things. Do things right, and you could land the job of your dreams. Do things wrong, and you could burn a bridge, hurt your reputation, and remain stuck.

Step #1:
Don't Let Misery Cloud Your Mind When It Comes to Jumping Ship

As you read this book, here's hoping you love your job so much you wouldn't even dream of leaving it, at least not for a while. But we live in the real would and know that sometimes jobs just don't work out as we had hoped. Perhaps you were promised a job that offered opportunities for growth, challenges, and learning—but you've been doing nothing but data entry for the past 18 months and you're bored out of your skull. Maybe you're overworked and underappreciated, and can't take another day reporting to the worst boss on the planet. Or perhaps you've realized that your job simply isn't something that you want to invest any more time in as a career choice, and you want to move on to something that better reflects what you want to do with your life. These are all perfectly understandable reasons for why you might want to look for a new job—after all, life is short, and it's only getting shorter. Why spend so much time doing something that isn't working?

Whether or not this is true, resist the urge to jump ship too quickly. Even if you're so miserable that you can think of nothing else but quitting, think long and hard about your next move before you head out the door. No matter how good your reasons, consider the fact that many of us have cloudy judgment when it comes to pulling the plug on our jobs, often because we're in a state of depression, fury, frustration, vengeance, or boredom when we're making these big decisions about quitting. As a result, decisions aren't made strategically but emotionally—not the best recipe for career success.

Nobody is suggesting that you stay in a job you hate, and leaving a job for a better opportunity is usually a very wise career move. Still, before you move on to greener pastures, keep a few things in mind:

- The fact is that the grass isn't always greener and every workplace has its share of good and bad. Lousy bosses and office politics exist everywhere, so don't assume that your job woes will disappear if you get hired someplace else. Be sure that your expectations are in check, so that you don't wind up leaving a job for something that doesn't really exist. In fact, if you're waiting on a raise,

promotion, or change in job responsibilities, don't assume that you'll be fast-tracked or get to bypass the waiting game by working someplace else.

- As the expression goes, "Wherever you go, there you
are." You can get a job offer on the other side of the
planet, but you're still going to be the one working in it.
If you hate the nine-to-five lifestyle, don't know what you
want to do with your life, or simply are feeling worried
and anxious about the future, those issues will be right
there with you, too, no matter where you work.

- You may not be marketable yet. If you quit your job before you've got enough time under your belt, chances are
that you also haven't necessarily built up a strong track
record and left your mark yet. Don't leave before you've
got some respectable accomplishments and tangible results to put on your résumé. Leaving too soon may hurt
your chances of being competitive against other job-
seekers at your age or level with more expertise than you.

- If you've worked at this job less than 18 months, the general rule of thumb is to suck it up and stick around for a
while. No matter how justified your reasons, quitting
within a few months or even a year is going to be a tough
sell when you're in the job market again. Unless you were
offered the dream job of the century or are in an absolutely unbearable situation, stick around long enough
to put some more time under your belt before you leave.

- Job-hopping gets a mixed review from recruiters and HR
in the marketplace. If your résumé lists too many jobs in
too short a time, you may raise some eyebrows. Quitting
too soon may send a message to employers that you can't

go the distance or that you leave when the going gets tough. If you have too many jobs on a résumé, employers may wonder if you will wind up doing the same thing to them. Can you really assure them that you won't bail out when things get difficult?

- You may be closer to the finish line than you think. As Ross Perot once put it, "Most people give up just when they're about to achieve success. They quit on the one-yard line." When you quit too early in the game, you won't reap the rewards that come with persevering and sticking it out, including better job titles, more money, and challenging, interesting work.

Knowing When It's Time to Leave

Clearly, leaving a job isn't quite the black-and-white issue that it may seem. Given that, when is it the right time to leave?

The short answer is this: Make sure that the job you walk into is going to do more for your long-term career goals than the one you have now. This goes way beyond being offered more money or having a nicer boss (though you'll want to be sure this new gig pays you what you're worth, certainly).

Instead, look for the aspects of the job that will really impact your career down the road and provide greater opportunities to gain marketable skills and experience. How will this new opportunity enhance your overall professionalism, expertise, and reputation? Will you work at a better-known organization, or with higher-level people, or bigger, brand-name clients? What about opportunities to grow and learn? Will you have more chances to gain training, certification, or education in your field with this new job?

If you were to compare all of the various aspects of your

current job (salary, benefits, responsibilities, commute, work environment/corporate culture, access to certain people, level of challenge, overall ability to make change, etc.) to the job that you are going for, how would each measure up? In other words, it isn't enough to leave a job just because it's not working out; you need to move into a job that will offer you more across the board than the current one does. Otherwise, stick where you are for the time being until you find something that brings greater opportunities to your career than what you've currently got.

Step #2:
Leave Your Job with Class and End on a High Note

How does the Johnny PayCheck song go: *"Take this job and shove it, I ain't workin' here no more . . ."*?

Given everything we've discussed, you may have determined that it really is time to move on. Happens all the time. However, what doesn't happen all the time is the graceful exit. Before you walk out the door, know how to leave the right way, so that the door is a revolving one, where you can continue to ask for help from your former colleagues and boss long after you've left.

Pick up a copy of the *Wall Street Journal,* and you'll read all kinds of stories about disgruntled, hurt employees who leave their jobs on a bad note. Heard the one about the guy who sent the angry email to everyone in the company when he quit? How about the one where the woman gave the boss a piece of her mind (and then some) before heading out the door? These people are out there, and you don't want to be one of them. I should know; I was one of them.

Here's the story: I landed a pretty plum job after graduate school. It was the kind of job everyone else from business school wanted, but I got, and I felt pretty darn superior about it (let's just say modesty wasn't my strong suit). Let's also just say that the job wasn't a good fit for various reasons, and I should have realized this before I accepted the offer. So why did I say yes when I should have said no? Hubris, my friends, plain and simple. I was a little dazzled and blinded by the prestigious company, and was more than a little flattered to think that they wanted little old *moi* to join them.

From the start, I was frustrated on the job. My boss had hired me to mow the lawn, but I wanted to build the Eiffel Tower. Had I been a bit more humble at the time, I would have realized that I didn't have a clue about how to build the Eiffel Tower, but as I said, modesty wasn't my strong suit.

Fortunately, I realized I was in the wrong place and managed to land another job which was a much better fit. Nonetheless, in an effort to be helpful (and perhaps vent my feelings a bit), I shared that I was frustrated and that I hadn't been "used to my fullest potential" during my exit interview with HR, a common practice at some companies. And on . . . and on . . . and on I went. Not my finest hour, I can assure you.

Is it wrong to offer constructive feedback during an exit interview? Certainly not. But it's one thing to be genuinely helpful and another to appear unappreciative (after all, they did hire me, train me, and pay me), immature, and whiny in any professional situation. Even worse, my boss, a nice guy, heard about my less-than-flattering comments and didn't appreciate them. I shot myself in the foot, and it took me a long time to repair the relationship with my boss and former employer. It didn't have to be that way.

The Seinfeld Way: End on a High Note

If you remember the TV show *Seinfeld,* you may also re-member the circumstances around which the highly rated television show came to an end. Despite the protests from NBC and fans everywhere for "one more season," Jerry Seinfeld decided to end the series on a high note: "I wanted the end to be from a point of strength. I wanted the end to be graceful."

When it comes to leaving a job, consider how you can adopt the *Seinfeld* approach, and end on a high note. Even if you're leaving under less-than-perfect circumstances, you can leave your job with strength and grace, too. If you take the alternate route, like I did, you hurt yourself in more ways than one. After all, the world is shrinking, and word about you does travel fast. When you leave on anything but a good note, you've burned a bridge—maybe the only one you've got. And when the bridge is gone, it can be hard to get to the place you want to go next.

How to end on a high note: The process begins long before your job ends

It may not always be possible to leave your job with your fans wanting more and the boss begging you to stay on. In fact, you and your boss may have mutually decided that your departure is a good thing, and you may be secretly thrilled to never have to set foot in that place again. Whatever the cir-cumstances, you'll want to do everything possible to leave on a great note—and that process begins long before you give your two weeks' notice.

Three months before departure: Set the process in motion

There are times when you may know several weeks or months in advance that you'll be leaving a job. This isn't always the case, but if you're heading off to graduate school or to travel, it isn't inconceivable that you'd know your anticipated departure date far in advance. Even if you aren't sure, don't hesitate to start taking steps now to leave on great terms.

- Start organizing all of your paperwork, online files, and anything else you've generated during your time at the office. Throw out junk, clean up, and straighten up. (By the way, this is a great thing to do a few times a year, regardless.) Take inventory of outstanding projects or incomplete work and start to tie up loose ends now.

- Imagine that your replacement will be walking into your role tomorrow: What can you do now to help him or her hit the ground running? Create a mini-training manual, write down instructions, provide lists of directions, tips, hints, or anything else that might be helpful.

- Despite everything, it's still business as usual. You aren't a second-semester senior in school who skips classes because it's almost graduation time. Keep performing at your job as well as you did when you first arrived.

- Depending on your job and relationship with your manager, you may want to consider sharing your plans to leave now. For example, if your job happens to be one that requires a unique or hard-to-find skill set, your boss may be stuck for several months after your departure while trying to find your replacement. By letting her know your plans in advance, you can offer to help recruit or train your replacement and won't leave anyone high and dry.

- Even if you know you're leaving the office at this stage, resist the urge to share the news with others, particularly if you haven't filled the boss in on your plans yet. People have different ways of reacting to their coworkers leaving: Your friends will miss you, others may be envious of you, and still others may not know whether they can count on you to really take work seriously for the next few weeks. Until you're very close to your departure date, keep things to yourself.

One month before departure: Take stock of what you've done

- If you've been with your company for a while, chances are that you've got some terrific accomplishments under your belt. If you haven't done this yet, create a formal document (spreadsheet, report, etc.) that outlines what you did and what the results were. Think of this as an embellished résumé to have for your records.

- Create a Portfolio of Accomplishments, where you compile some samples of your best work and organize them in a three-ring binder or something else that you can take with you. You portfolio might contain brochures you've written, spreadsheets you've designed, even emails from your boss acknowledging a job well done. How to use your portfolio? You wouldn't necessarily march into a job interview and open it to page three, but you never know when you might be asked to produce examples of work you've done. For instance, I once applied for a public relations position where I was asked to submit five samples of actual press releases I had written. Because I had the permission of my former employer to share my past work (see more on this below), I was able to use my portfolio to showcase my experience.

Read this three times: Only take this step with the permission of the organization. After all, that work belongs to them—they paid for it. Don't walk out the office door with a single copy of anything you've done until you've absolutely gotten the OK. You might have worked on information that's confidential or proprietary, and your organization doesn't want anyone else laying their eyes on it. In fact, if you do take files, documents, or anything else without permission, your company can have you arrested for stealing, so don't do it.

- Once again, consider giving your notice now if you can. You aren't technically obligated to tell anyone you're leaving at this juncture, but it may score you some points for the same reasons listed earlier. Plus, you don't want to surprise anyone or leave your team in the lurch, so it may be time to ask to meet with the boss to discuss some "career choices" you've been making. Use your best judgment here—if you're in the kind of situation where it's only going to make things more difficult, best to stay mum on quitting for the time being.

Two weeks before departure: Put on the finishing touches

- You aren't technically obligated under the law to tell your employer you're leaving now, but it's the right thing to do, so don't wait another day before giving your official notice—and do this in writing and in person. Give a copy to your boss, HR, and anyone else who was involved in bringing you on board.

- Now that your departure is officially out of the bag, you can share your news with others, including coworkers, supervisors, and clients, discreetly. Whether you choose to let people know in person, over the phone, or in a group email with your future contact information, be extremely gracious and offer thanks and appreciation for the time you had with them.

- Be sure to also express your gratitude to your manager. In addition to your letter of resignation, send another letter to the boss right before your last days on the job and express your thanks here, too. Thank your boss for the opportunity she's given you, tell her how much you've learned from her, and express your appreciation for the chance to be on her team.

- Don't leave your job without lining up references, even if you've already got another job. Ask a mix of those who have supervised you, including your manager, if they'd be willing to serve as references on your behalf for future job searches or other professional situations. Clients, vendors, or other people outside of your organization may also be good choices—just be sure to ask people who know you and have seen you in action. Keep in mind that references may not be able to share more about you than your title, dates employed, and final salary level because of employer liability, but nonetheless, pick references who have only terrific things to say. If you're not sure, leave them off your list.

- Along with references, you may want to consider asking for letters of recommendation in writing from key people where appropriate. Offer to draft the letter for them, ask for it on the company letterhead, and don't wait too long before getting these in hand. As great as you are, people are busy and memories fade. For instance, a former supervisor from an early job agreed to write a letter of recommendation on my behalf when I applied to graduate school several years later, and asked me for something in writing to jog his memory of specific projects I had worked on while in his employ. I did that, and also forwarded him the previous letter he had written on my behalf. This made his life easier when writing my new recommendation because he didn't have to create something from scratch, and also produced a stronger letter, because he was able to remember important details that he may have otherwise forgotten.

- Remember, life and work demands still continue for your coworkers, so don't turn your departure into a big production. Sending out a group email with your contact information to coworkers or other people you've worked with is fine (though be sure to conceal recipients' names on the message for privacy reasons), and there is nothing wrong with your coworkers wanting to take you out for a goodbye lunch, for instance. The key here is discretion and professionalism: As long as your departure doesn't turn into the workplace version of Cher's Farewell Tour (which lasted over three years), you'll be fine.

The last impression: Handling yourself during the exit interview

If you think first impressions count, consider the last impression: It's forever! Think about it: With first impressions, you've got opportunities to make up for any blunders or mistakes you made along the way. But if your mistake is made right before you exit the lobby of your office building, it's going to be much harder to erase that image from people's minds. And the last impression that really counts, as far as work is concerned, is usually the exit interview.

What exactly is an exit interview? If you've never been through one before, you aren't necessarily missing much. From an HR perspective, an exit interview is a learning opportunity, giving your employer a chance to find out why you're leaving and learn how to fix things for next time. From an employee's perspective, these sessions may seem like a case of too little, too late, particularly if you're asked common questions like *"Why are you deciding to leave the company?" "Were you happy with your salary and benefits?"* For these reasons, it isn't a big surprise that more and more companies are getting rid of the exit interview altogether.

Nonetheless, if are participating in one, you may be tempted to unload, pour your heart out, or simply vent about what a witch your boss was. Don't do this. Even if the HR rep seems sympathetic, this is risky for you and your reputation. Bite your lip if you must, but don't, repeat, don't turn your exit interview into drama or a work-bashing session. Instead, answer questions politely and briefly, and leave. Don't stick around long enough to say something you'll regret.

After you've left: Make the effort to keep in touch
Once you've said your goodbyes and shed a tear or two (or perhaps yelped out shrieks of joy), you're ready to move on. Even as you enter a new job and new phase in your career, don't forget to keep in touch with your former manager, supervisors, even clients. In the spirit of relationship-building, this is a perfect opportunity to increase your network, so make the most of your ties.

To some, this may come very naturally, and you'd think nothing of giving your former boss a phone call or email anytime. For others, you may need a few more reminders.

Every few months, make the effort to get in touch with your former coworkers and managers to say hello, update them on your progress, and see what they are working on. Not only does this strengthen your relationships, but it keeps you viewed positively in their minds—a smart move, particularly when some of these people may be acting as references, and can also be sources of future opportunities and jobs for you. After all, they already know you and have seen you in action, so put in the effort to maintain your connection with them. Drop your old boss a note out of the blue and let her know how much you appreciated what you learned from her—even if you didn't show it at the time. (P.S. I did this once—and I can't tell you how much my old boss loved it. After receiving my letter, she called me up to thank me, and we spent several minutes on the phone chatting about life and work. Another unexpected benefit of my note? It put me back on my former manager's radar screen and reminded her of what I was capable of doing. As a result, she referred two pieces of business to me—not bad, and all of that from one little note.)

Do yourself and your career a favor and end every professional encounter the right way. You worked hard to start your job on the right note, so do the same when you're leaving, too. And, if you blow it, try again. It's never too late to repair a broken bridge and build a new one.

Step #3:
Begin Your Next Career Chapter with a Job Search that Brings Results

Whether you've already left your job or are starting to consider a career move, embarking on a job search is a serious undertaking. As the saying goes, "Looking for a job is a full-time job." That's the truth: Between your résumé, cover letters, networking, interviewing, following up, and more, you could easily be up to your eyeballs in work. If you're currently employed, this is where things get a bit sticky. After all, if you spend your days working on that résumé or stepping out for three-hour lunches to interview for a job, you'll probably get caught, fast—not to mention the fact that you're being paid to do a job, not look for a new one.

When it comes to conducting a job search, manage yourself carefully. Keep your work for after hours and on weekends, and resist the urge to use a company computer, copier, email address, or anything else for your job-search activities. And while you're at it, manage your time carefully, too. The fact is that a job search often takes longer than we think, particularly if you don't have the world's greatest résumé or are trying to change careers from one field to another, so don't try to rush this project.

Here's the good news: It can be done. Put in the time, effort, and work, and you can land a job that you'll be proud of. Put in the practice, and you can become a sharp, smooth interviewee. Ask the right questions, and you can wind up with valuable information and feedback that can make a big difference in your next moves.

Here's the bad news: If you think that landing a job is as simple as point-click-wait for the phone to ring, think again. Too many people conduct a job search in this passive fashion, by surfing the Web, applying for jobs online, and then hoping that someone will call them. Good luck. Because it's so darn easy to look for jobs in this way, everybody does it, which is why many of us wind up empty-handed or frustrated when applying for jobs online. The moral of the story? Use the Internet as a job-search tool, but don't put all your eggs in that basket.

Starting Your Job Search:
What Do You Want to Be When You Grow Up?

If it takes more than the Internet to land you a job, what exactly do you need to do? Start from the beginning by asking yourself a simple—and difficult—question: *"What do I really want to do?"* Imagine getting into a taxi and saying to the driver, "Take me anywhere." Pretty risky strategy, wouldn't you say? Sure, the driver could take you somewhere terrific, but you might wind up in the middle of Lousyville, USA, too.

The same is true for your job search: If you don't know where you want to go next, you're taking a chance. After all, if you aren't sure where to put your job-search energy, it can be tempting to send a résumé off to anything that seems halfway decent. Don't believe the myth that applying to lots of jobs keeps your options open. In fact, by submitting your résumé to anything with a heartbeat, you appear unfocused, and take important time and energy away from landing a job that your really do want.

Make the Call: Pick a Focus, Make a Decision, and Get Going on Your Job Search

Here's a dilemma many job-seekers face: We know what we dislike doing or what we don't want as a career. The problem? We get stuck when it comes to figuring out what we actually *do* want.

If you're feeling stuck, check out our tips below to get your job search moving along and on its way.

- *TIP #1:* Don't spend the rest of your life figuring out what you want to do with the rest of your life—you don't have time for that. Even if you really have no idea what you want to be when you grow up, go with your best guess. Your next job won't be your last job, after all, and what's the worst thing that can happen? You make the wrong choice, which doesn't leave you any worse off than you are now, anyway.

- *TIP #2:* Only apply for jobs you really, truly are excited about. If you don't love it, don't apply for it. Now is the time to become the person you want to be and stop applying for jobs that you know, in your heart of hearts, you just don't care about.

- *TIP #3:* If you really don't know where to begin, take a self-assessment test online through a well-respected company to give you some ideas. You'll have to pay some money, but it may be well worth it. Assessments are helpful self-awareness tools designed to give you a sense of where your talents rest and what careers or job functions would make best use of your talents. (One note: These things aren't perfect. You might find out that you'd make a great monk, when the celibate lifestyle isn't necessarily your thing. Still, press on—you may get some helpful insights.)

- *TIP #4:* Keep a journal and write down thoughts, ideas, or anything of interest. If you read about a cool job, make a note of it. If you come across an interesting article that featured someone successful, write that down, too. After all, these interesting things that you come across are clues, giving you insight into what really makes you tick, so keep track of what naturally seems to grab you.

The Only Way to Know about Something Is to Do It

Imagine going into a clothing store because you want to buy a pair of jeans. If you were serious about buying a pair, would you pull something from the shelf, stick your big toe in a pant leg, and proclaim, "Nope! They're all wrong for me." I doubt it. Instead, you'd probably go into a dressing room and actually try on the jeans, wouldn't you? You'd zip them up, dance in front of the mirror, or do whatever you needed to do to make sure you really had something that fit you.

When it comes to figuring out what you want to do, your process isn't so different from buying jeans. Too often, we make big decisions about jobs we think we'd like or dislike, but we actually haven't had any of them before. It's almost as if we stick our big toe into an idea and say, "No! Insurance could never be for me!" even though we know nothing about the insurance industry or whether we'd enjoy it. All too often, our ideas about jobs aren't based on our actual experience, but come from something we saw on TV, something our cousin once told us, or something based on a notion we had at some point but really can't remember, anyway.

If you want to know whether something really is right or not for you, you've got to actually try it on, just like a pair of jeans. Most of us skip this important step in our lives, which is why so many of us wind up in careers that are dissatisfying or simply wrong for us—it's because we never bothered to try them on first.

This isn't to suggest that you get an internship for every profession that's out there, nor does it mean that you can't trust your own instincts. After all, I feel pretty safe in saying that I would not enjoy a career as a proctologist, for instance. But if you think you might enjoy marketing or teaching, give yourself an opportunity to experiment in the role. Volunteer to teach an ESL class in your community, for example, or offer to do a marketing project for a local nonprofit for free.

Try on your career before you jump into it by taking action that allows you to experiment in the role you'd like to assume. In doing so, you'll gain some insight, experience, and really see for yourself whether something fits you or doesn't. Go beyond reading about interesting jobs or conducting lots of informational interviews as your main sources of information. These are great ways to network and learn more about opportunities, but, ultimately, they may not help you see what really fits.

Step #4:
Develop Marketing Materials that Break through the Clutter and Get Noticed

Once you've really figured out where to focus your time and energy when it comes to a job search, your job-search life becomes significantly less complicated. After all, now you've got a broad strategy, an overarching principal to guide all of your next moves, including how you write a résumé, cover letter, and anything else that will help you land a job, including emails or any other form of communication.

Unfortunately, you'll still have to put in some serious time as a job-seeker, because no strategy, no matter how good, can write a résumé or cover letter for you. No focus, no matter how clear, is going to be the one networking, making phone calls, interviewing, and following up. No, you've got to do that, and the sooner you get started, the better.

If You're a Job-Seeker, You've Landed a Job, Whether You Realize It or Not

Whether you know it or not, if you're looking for a job, you're already employed. What do I mean? Welcome to the world of sales. Even if you haven't worked a day in months or are currently employed by Greenpeace, you need to get comfortable with the idea of selling your skills, talents, and expertise in the marketplace if you want to land a job in the next 50 years.

As we stated earlier, selling yourself isn't about becoming fake or phony, but let's acknowledge the fact that in most cases, the phone isn't ringing off the hook with job offers for you. If you want the phone to ring, you've got to make others aware of how you can contribute to the success of their organizations. And, friends, that's sales, 100 percent.

For Job-Seekers, Selling Begins on Paper

Whether you're writing a résumé, cover letter, or email, your ability to communicate with insight and impact is critical when applying for jobs. After all, busy professionals—including recruiters and hiring managers—are inundated with emails, résumés, and other materials on a daily basis. The result? Long emails, boring letters, and unprofessional résumés get discarded, deleted, and ignored.

If you want your résumé and cover letter to get read, be remembered, and stand out above the noise and competition, avoid the common mistakes that many job-seekers make.

Mistake #1: You confused them
Let's imagine a typical job-search scenario: You've read about an interesting job online, so you whip up a cover let-

ter, dash off your résumé, and you wait by the phone (or computer) for some kind of acknowledgment or reply from a recruiter about what's to come. Unfortunately, the phone doesn't ring and you're left wondering what you did wrong.

Consider this possibility: You were confusing. Maybe you applied for a sales position, but you also mentioned that you'd "be open to a position in marketing or finance" in your cover letter. Or perhaps you have job experience in everything from teaching English to baking pastries—and it's all on your résumé.

THE SOLUTION: CLARITY. When you give too much information about yourself, your professional history, your future career goals, or anything else for that matter, you run the risk of confusing people. As much as we'd like to think people read what we write (she writes, hopefully) and listen to what we say, chances are, they don't. People are busy and time is limited. Your job is to be direct, clear, and get to the point—fast.

Before you send out a résumé or pick up the phone, ask yourself this question: *"Above everything else, what is the one thing I want the reader of this email/résumé/cover letter to know about me?"* Think about how you can edit—or even remove—everything on paper that doesn't fit your "one thing" requirement. For instance, if you're dying for a position in investment banking, do you really need five bullet points on your résumé about your work as an English teacher? The more information you throw at somebody, the less likely it will be read and really remembered.

Mistake #2: You bored them
Busy professionals—including recruiters and hiring managers—are swamped with information. Consider the hundreds of résumés, emails, and phone calls they have to field on any given day, not to mention the number of candidates they

meet and interview in any given week, and you see how crit-ical it is to break through the clutter and capture their atten-tion in a professional way. Bore them and, chances are, you'll lose them.

THE SOLUTION: OFFER MEANINGFUL INFORMATION THAT MATTERS TO THE READER. If you want your résumé and cover letter to stand out above the noise and competition, your written materials must be concise, clear, and deliver meaningful messages that grab the reader. Leave out the clichés like "I'm a team player," "I think outside the box," or "I'm a hard worker." Even if these things are true about you, everybody writes this stuff, and these kinds of descriptors are just too broad and sweeping to really deliver any mean-ing, anyway. Plus, do *you* really believe it when someone else tells you that they are a "hard worker"? If you're like most people, you'll believe it when you see it.

Recruiters are the same way. If you really are a hard worker and you want to say so, then you also need to prove it. Don't write it unless you're also prepared to offer a clear, concise example about a time when you really put the pedal to the metal. In fact, whenever you write anything about yourself, always be ready to offer up a story, an example, or some other evidence that truly demonstrates you are who you say you are.

Mistake #3: You didn't tailor for them
When it comes to your résumé and cover letter (though I prefer "marketing materials"), one size does not fit all. Writing a powerful résumé and a cover letter that packs a punch aren't exactly a walk in the park. This stuff takes time and effort, which is why many of us don't relish the thought of going through the process more than once. The result? We send the exact same résumé and cover letter (with a change of name or address here or there) to each and every job we

apply for. But this isn't smart: When you don't take the time to tailor your résumé and cover letter for distinct positions, you dilute the strength of your résumé and will have a tougher time competing against others who have a stronger focus and message than yours.

THE SOLUTION: POSITION YOUR RÉSUMÉ AND COVER LETTER EACH AND EVERY TIME YOU SEND THEM OUT. I'm not suggesting you reinvent the wheel or create an entirely new set of materials for every job that's out there. Instead, look carefully at the job description before you click send and make sure that your information truly reflects the needs of the employer and how you can best contribute to those needs. Yes, this is extra effort, but it's not always easy to get a foot in a door and a shot at your dream job. Make the most of every opportunity and take the extra time to really customize your marketing materials—it may make the difference between an interview for you or someone else.

Step #5:
Fix What Isn't Working to Land a Job You'll Love

Got a fever? Take some aspirin. Sore throat? Perhaps some bed rest will help. Looking for a job but still haven't found one? The remedy for this one is considerably trickier. As you know by now, landing a job isn't as easy as having a great résumé and cover letter—that's only the beginning. There's interviewing, networking, following up—and doing this over and over until you land an offer or two.

What if you aren't getting offers? What if your résumé isn't generating interest? Then what? I'll tell you one remedy that doesn't work: Panic and beat yourself up for not getting millions of job offers (or even one). And the remedy where you spend a lot of time hoping, wishing, thinking, and praying that you'll just somehow magically land a job without having to network or make phone calls? That doesn't work too well, either.

If you're looking for a remedy to unemployment or simply want to understand why your job search hasn't resulted in anything yet, the answer isn't always as simple as taking a couple of aspirin. In fact, one of the reasons why it's so hard to figure out your individual job-search challenges is because you haven't always diagnosed the problem correctly.

In other words, if your job search isn't going along as smashingly as you would like, stop for a minute and take your job-search temperature. Give yourself a moment to slow down, get honest with yourself, and really figure out what isn't working for you. When you assess and diagnose your situation accurately, you can pinpoint the specific job-search areas you need to work on and better identify solutions for doing so.

How do you take your job-search temperature? Review the past few months of your job-search life and consider where you've most often stumbled.

If you're like most other job-seekers, your temperature reading probably revealed one of the following diagnoses.

Diagnosis #1: Time

More often than not, job-seekers will diagnose "time" as the problem in their job-search situation. Quite simply, you haven't put in enough time on a regular basis to make any real progress.

This could be because you're putting all of your time into your current job or other responsibilities. It could also be because you dread the job search and have procrastinated and put off the necessary tasks of working on a résumé, networking, practicing interviewing skills, and so on.

In some cases, job-seekers underestimate how long a job search can actually take, particularly for career changes, people with less job experience, or those of us who are a little rusty when it comes to writing a strong résumé or dazzling them in the interview.

CONSIDER THE REMEDY: Unfortunately, time management isn't one of those issues that we can slap a Band-Aid on to fix. We each have 168 hours in a week to spend however we choose. Do you choose to spend a chunk of that time on your job search and career . . . or not? The choice is yours, and nobody can make the job search a priority—a top priority—but you.

Obviously, we're not knocking the importance of managing the responsibilities of your current job or anything else. But if you're finding that everything else comes before the job search, or that you're so busy doing other stuff that you can't spare a few measly hours a week for your job search, take a deep breath and remind yourself why you want a career change in the first place. Envision your mean boss or your measly bank account whenever you're tempted to turn on *American Idol* instead of working on your job search. Do what you have to do to make this a priority—may I remind you this is your life we are talking about?

Diagnosis #2: Interviews

While time management is an issue we all struggle with, your temperature reading may reveal something different. If you're like a lot of job-seekers, you might discover that you are putting in the time, but you simply aren't getting selected for a lot of interviews. We all run into this issue on occasion, but if you haven't landed a job interview since Bill Clinton was in office, this could be your temperature talking.

CONSIDER THE REMEDY: First, I'm going to guess that your résumé needs some work. After all, it is your résumé's job to get you the interview. Your résumé has to **blaze**—it's got to be sharp. Use strong language to sell your accomplishments, use numbers to quantify those accomplishments, and don't be afraid to be bold in that cover letter.

What if you've got the perfect résumé and you still aren't getting interviews?

Consider your channels of distribution. For example, are you only applying for jobs on campus or online? If so, you're making things tough on yourself, because when you only apply for jobs through these passive channels, you're competing against lots and lots of people for a single opportunity. Those are tough odds, where a fantastic résumé may get buried or lost in the clutter.

The solution? Get out from behind the computer screen and start networking. When you network in a way where you are focusing on giving (not taking) and building long-term relationships (not one-time meetings or phone calls), you'll begin to meet people who can put your résumé in the right hands. (For more on relationship-building, reread the networking chapter in this book.)

What if you have the perfect résumé and you are networking day and night—and you are STILL not getting interviews?

If this is you, I want you to consider the types of jobs for which you are applying. Are you applying for everything and anything out there, even if you really don't have the background or experience? Or, consider the fact that you may be overshooting, applying for jobs for which you really aren't qualified. For instance, you may be seeking opportunities with top-tier consulting firms (which typically hire only from Ivy League or other top schools). If this is you, ask yourself if you are applying for jobs for which you are legitimately qualified and where you really have an honest shot.

Diagnosis #3: Offers

As many of us have experienced, it is one thing to get the job interview, but it's entirely another to land an offer. This is the trickiest job-search diagnosis, because for each of you reading right now, there's probably a different reason why you may have not received a job offer after interviewing for a position. Still, let's take a shot at it.

CONSIDER THE REMEDY: First, you and I know that you've got to really, really show your enthusiasm, expertise, and confidence during the interview. To do this, you MUST practice interviewing. Do this often—especially if you're interviewing for jobs in a language or culture different from your own. How to practice interviewing? It's easy to videotape your mock interview and then review it with a professional. Get feedback on your responses, on your outfit, on your mannerisms. Do this a few times—you'll be amazed at how much you can improve.

What if you've practiced and practiced and you're still not getting offers?

Make sure you're really able to talk someone through your résumé in a way that doesn't just give a timeline or facts but *sells who you are.* Practice answers to commonly asked interview questions (including "Take me through your résumé" or "Tell me why you're interested in our company and this position") so that you are constantly showcasing your expertise and enthusiasm throughout your responses.

Better yet, write out a script for each answer and rehearse out loud. Don't worry about sounding unnatural in a job interview—you'll simply sound polished and confident, and you won't run the risk of forgetting important things that you meant to say, but didn't because you were caught off guard, unprepared, or nervous.

But what if you are a very, very strong interviewer and you're STILL not getting offers?

If you think this is you, you've got to *ask for feedback* from the recruiters or hiring managers who interviewed you but did not offer you jobs. Not everyone will share this with you, but you'll be surprised at how many candid answers you will receive.

While I was getting my MBA, I was turned down by a large company for a job opportunity. Naturally, I was convinced I was sheer perfection in the interview and couldn't fathom why I didn't get a job offer. So I contacted the hiring manager who interviewed me and was told that I had "poor eye contact." Ouch . . . but if I hadn't asked, I wouldn't have known, and I worked on the eye contact. Do yourself a favor and ask diplomatically, so that you aren't making the same interview mistakes over and over.

Taking your job-search temperature isn't always easy, but it is necessary. After all, if you don't know what's wrong, how can you fix it? Figure out what you need to fix, and get better soon.

The Job Search Requires Endurance: Get in It to Win It

No matter how terrific you are, it's inevitable that you'll hit a roadblock or two along your job-search journey. Call me a crazy optimist, but I'd like to think that most of us won't let a few measly rejections get in the way of pursuing an opportunity that really matters to us. Often, particularly in the face of rejection, it's easy to lose faith, and one no too many can let the doubt creep in. "Maybe I'm crazy for thinking this would work," you despair. "Maybe I'm going for a job that's just way too competitive," you wonder. "Maybe I'm a total idiot for thinking this would ever work out at all," you sigh.

You've heard it before, but allow me to repeat this obvious truth: If you don't believe in yourself, who will? Remember, you're in sales now, and if you can't get 100 percent behind your product—whether that product is your skills, talents, or experience on a résumé—then why should anybody else?

Deep down, if you aren't quite sure whether you've got what it takes, remind yourself that *nobody has to know that but you.* With confidence, you believe in you—and getting one step closer to your goal becomes a heck of a lot easier. With a real belief in yourself and your abilities, you are able to better withstand the rejections that come with the territory of trying to get ahead in the world. Heck, you might even become one of those kooks who begins to like hearing no— after all, one more no is closer to a yes, right?

Leaving a job with class isn't easy, and conducting a job search that delivers results isn't any easier, but these are two activities where a little effort goes a long way. When it comes to your career, leaving on the right foot helps you start your next journey with everything you need to make it a successful one.

It Isn't What You Know . . . It's What You Do with What You Know that Counts

CONGRATULATIONS! You did it—you took an important, proactive step in getting your career off on the right foot. After all, the fact that you bought this book and made it this far indicates that you're serious about your professional life and want to make the most of it. That's smart. After all, when you consider the fact that most of us spend the majority of our adult lives working, it only makes sense to do the best we can with this huge chunk of our lives.

And that's why it isn't enough to simply read this book, as good a first step as that is. Learning the ropes to have the kind of career you want isn't always easy; as you've read, it takes plenty of thought, hard work, and real commitment to learning and growing. Not to mention time, effort, late nights, and early mornings, which is probably why so many of us don't wind up happy in our careers: In 2005, one Conference Board study reported that over half of all

Americans are growing increasingly unhappy with their jobs. In fact, only 14 percent reported being "very satisfied," and 25 percent of employees are just "showing up to collect a paycheck."

You Don't Have Time to Be Miserable

Let's face it: Life is too short to be unhappy in your job. It doesn't mean that every day at work is a nonstop party, or that you won't have days where even the best of jobs drives you crazy. This also isn't to suggest that work matters most in the universe; chances are that you may care a heck of a lot more about your parents, your boyfriend, your friends, and your cat than you do about work in the first place, anyway. But the fact still remains that for many of us, work will take up an enormous amount of our time and energy for a large part of our lives, and that doesn't even include the amount of time spent worrying, fretting, venting, and obsessing about our jobs when we're *not* at work. The moral of the story? If you're unhappy at work, you're unhappy a lot of the time—and who has time for that?

Put Yourself on the Path to Success: A Few Final Thoughts

The secret to getting out of a career mess? Take to heart an unspoken rule that you already know: You've got to get in the race to win it. Here are some final thoughts on how to start.

Talk Is Cheap

If there is something you want to do, quit thinking about it and start doing something instead, according to Dan Goor, comedy writer for the Conan O'Brien show. Like many of his close friends in college, Dan wanted to be a comedy writer after graduation. Less than two years after graduating, most of his fellow classmates had moved on to other jobs or plans, discouraged by the difficulty and rejection that comes with pursing a career in writing. While Dan also experienced rejection and unemployment, he still kept submitting writing samples and working on his ideas, day after day. "So many people talk about wanting to do something, but most people won't really take the action that is necessary. Or they quit when things get tough," says Dan.

If you're serious about pursuing your goals, then you must be willing to take action again and again. Resolve not to let challenges get the best of you. Instead, remind yourself on a daily basis why your goals matters to you, and keep taking one small step at a time toward achieving them.

Failure Is Bound to Happen—the Key Is How You Handle It

If you're going to have a career you love, then running into the "F" word is inevitable. No, dealing with failure (yes, that "F" word) isn't always pretty, but we know that it's just part of living.

But it's one thing to know intellectually that failure is OK and quite another to really *feel* that it is OK. Sure, sometimes failing at something is nature's way of telling us to get a clue about ourselves, and we'd be foolish if we didn't try to understand why we failed at something. Still, when the going

gets tough and you strike out, don't throw in the towel or
become convinced that your setback is a sign from God that
you shouldn't be doing what you're doing.

Consider a conversation between the actor Jack Black
and a younger actor from his movie *School of Rock,* where
they discuss how the typical actor faces 19 rejections before
he lands a role. "I've definitely not gotten the part way more
times than I've gotten the part . . . so if you get one out of,
like, 20 auditions, you're actually doing really good," said
Black during the DVD's extra features. Remember that no
one is counting your mishaps except you and that it only
takes one sale, one job offer, or, in his case, one starring
movie role to make all the difference.

Listen with Only One Ear

Ever gotten advice that made you feel lousy? Someone's
"helpful" criticism, advice, or other expertise doesn't necessarily have to spell failure for you. Consider the stories outlined in Steve Young's book *Great Failures of the Extremely
Successful,* where he shares dozens of examples of successful people refusing to let others' beliefs and attitudes get in
their way. For instance, Young shares a story about Elvis
Presley, who was fired from the Grand Ole Opry after only
one performance and told by the manager, "You ain't goin'
nowhere, son. Better get y'all job back drivin' a truck." There
are countless examples of people who heard brutal criticism,
got fired, lost the deal—and kept going anyway. The moral
of the story? We need to half-listen to these messages of criticism or failure, determine they are *not* signs from God to
throw in the towel, and just stick to our plan.

Persist, Because the Rewards Are Worth It

Let's face it: Learning the ropes of your workplace isn't just about getting a promotion or a raise, though those things are certainly important to life on the job. Instead, by taking the time to create the kind of professional life you're excited about, you're being challenged to do more than show up, do your work, and call it a day. Instead, you're really being asked to reach beyond the boundaries of who you are now in order to become something greater to your coworkers, your organization, and even to yourself. You're being asked to take the life you have today and kick it up a notch or two on the job, so that you'll like your life tomorrow, too.

This kind of personal and professional evolution isn't exactly spelled out for us in job descriptions or interviews, and it may not be what you agreed to do when you signed on the dotted line. After all, taking the steps outlined in this book requires commitment, risk, and ongoing effort, and there are no guarantees, so why bother?

Sure, at times, you may feel like you're the only one working late instead of going to happy hour, or you might wonder if you're crazy to use vacation days to attend a professional seminar instead of heading to Florida in January, but as long as you understand why your goals matter to you, persistence will come naturally, at least most of the time. After all, this is your *life* we're talking about. And while there is no magic bullet or easy answer when it comes to career success, consider the alternative: When you settle for less in your job, you settle for less in your life, and if you've ever had a job that you didn't feel good about, you know that's the truth. If learning the ropes of the workplace will bring you closer to the rewards of having raises, promotions, *and* the career and life that you really want, then don't wait another minute. Start now.

About the Author

ELIZABETH FREEDMAN, M.B.A., is the author of *The MBA Student's Job-Seeking Bible* and a 2005 finalist for College Speaker of the Year, awarded by the Association for the Promotion of Campus Activities. She runs a Boston-based communications and career development firm that works with corporations to help their new professionals look sharp, sound smart, and succeed on the job. Clients include Proctor & Gamble/The Gillette Company, Pricewaterhouse-Coopers, and the Thomson Corporation. Throughout the year, Elizabeth delivers programs to college students and employees across the country on the areas of work and career success. She lives in Natick, Massachusetts, with her husband and two children. Her website is www.elizabeth freedman.com.